COMMENTARY ON
THE DHARMA OF TIMELESS ZEN

COMMENTARY ON
THE DHARMA OF TIMELESS ZEN

Published by Seoul Selection
4199 Campus Dr., Suite 550, Irvine, CA 92612, USA
Phone: 949-509-6584 Fax: 949-509-6599
Email: publisher@seoulselection.com
Website: www.seoulselection.com
Printed in the Republic of Korea

ISBN: 978-1-62412-039-8

Library of Congress Control Number: 2015947125

COMMENTARY ON
THE DHARMA OF TIMELESS ZEN

from *The Principal Book of Won-Buddhism*

Seoul Selection

◯ Contents

PREFACE

I was visited one day by a younger *Won*-Buddhist who asked me to do a commentary on the "Dharma of Timeless Zen," something along the same lines as my *Commentary on the Methods of Seated Meditation.* "Isn't most of that already contained in *Class of the Mind?*" I asked. But what this person was asking for was a commentary focused specifically on the text.

After seeing him off, I thought about it for a while before deciding that I could not very well turn down a rare request like that from one of my juniors. I spent a few days pondering and reverently reading the text of the dharma instruction, and I finally saw the need for a commentary and began to write. Though the text might seem ordinary in content, it contained a condensed version of everything from the beginnings of Zen to the ultimate stage. It gave only the broadest principles of the methods of Timeless Zen, so it seemed that I needed to explain at least some of the different related cases. And so it was this that I began writing.

In my efforts to avoid as much as possible going beyond the scope of the text, I attempted merely to flesh out a bit some of the interconnected elements and methodological practicalities.

Yet if you are seeking to approach the essence of this practice, I believe that you may be able to easily grasp the path of practice when you combine the Dharma of Fixed-Term Training and Dharma of Daily Training given in the *Principal Book of Won-Buddhism* with the Dharma of Keeping a Diary. As such, I decided simply to add some minor explanations in the hopes that readers would consult the training dharma portions of the *Principal Book*'s "Practice" chapter for the specifics.

I hope that this commentary serves as a guide to beginners who are looking for the path of practice, and I hope that countless companions with the unequaled power of great enlightenment, as well as countless gifted and great bodhisattvas of the Way without form, can be produced through this, our dharma of self-cultivation.

TEXT OF THE
"DHARMA OF TIMELESS ZEN"
BY SECTION

I. The Purpose of Zen

As a rule, Zen is a practice that leads to the achievement of freedom of mind by awakening to one's own nature, which is originally free from discrimination or attachment. Since time immemorial, those who have been determined to achieve the great Way have all practiced Zen.

II. The Dharma of Mahāyāna Meditation

If people intend to practice genuine Sŏn, they first should take true voidness as the substance and marvelous existence as the function and, externally, be unmoving like Mount T'ai when in contact with the myriad of sensory conditions, and, internally, keep the mind unsullied, like empty space. Let the mind function so that it is not acting even in action and not resting even at rest. If we do so, then there will be no discrimination that is separate from purity, so that the functioning of the six sense organs will accord with the self-nature of the void and calm, numinous awareness. This is what is called Mahāyāna meditation, the method of practice in which we progress in concert through the Threefold Study.

III. When and Where We Can Practice Zen

It says in a sūtra, "Give rise to a mind that, even while responding, does not abide anywhere." This is precisely the great dharma of practice that remains unmoved amid the myriad of sensory conditions. This dharma may seem extremely difficult, but if only we come to understand in detail the methods of practice, then even a farmer wielding a hoe can practice Sŏn, as can a carpenter wielding a hammer, a clerk using an abacus, and an official seeing to an administrative matter; and we can practice Sŏn even while going about or staying at home. What need is there to bother with choosing a specific place and with talking about action or rest?

IV. The Reality of Zen

However, for people who are first beginning to practice Zen, the mind is not easily controlled according to their wishes; it is like training an ox where, if the reins of the mind are dropped even for a moment, it will instantly harm one's commitment to the Way. Therefore, if you keep exerting yourself without letting go of that spirit that is ready to fight to the bitter end no matter how alluring the sensory conditions you face may be, the mind will gradually become tamed and you will reach a state where the mind will do what you wish. Each and every time you are in contact with a sensory condition, do not forget to keep the thought in mind that an opportunity for practice has arrived, always taking a suitable measure of whether or not you are affected by that sensory condition. Thus, once there is a gradual increase in instances of behavior in which the mind does what you wish, you may from time to time let yourself be put in situations that you normally would find extremely attractive or abhorrent. If the mind is moved as before, then your commitment to the Way is immature; but if it is unmoved, then you will know that this is proof that your commitment to the Way is ripening. However, at the very time that you realize that the mind is unmoving, do not let down your guard, for it is unmoving through your employing the mental powers, rather than naturally unmoving. The mind has been well tamed only when it is unmoving even if left unguarded.

V. The Results of Zen Practice

If you continue for a long time practicing Zen so as to put an end to all the defilements and achieve freedom of mind, then you will be centered like an iron pillar and defended from the outside like a stone wall so that neither wealth nor status nor honor nor glory can coax the mind, nor can anyone use weapons or authority to make the mind submit. Practicing all dharmas in this manner, you will never be enticed or obstructed, and even while residing in this dusty world, you will constantly attain hundreds and thousands of samādhis. Once you reach this stage, the entire world will be transformed into the one genuine realm of reality, and right and wrong, good and evil, and all the defiled and pure dharmas will become the single taste of ghee. This state is called the gateway of nonduality. Freedom in birth and death, liberation from the cycle of rebirths, and the ultimate bliss of the pure land all emerge through this gateway.

VI. Prejudices Regarding Zen

Recently, groups that practice Zen have thought that Zen is extremely difficult. There are many who hold that it is impossible to do for someone who has a family or who pursues an occupation and that you can only practice Zen by entering into the mountains and sitting quietly. This view derives from their ignorance of the great dharma, in which all dharmas are nondual. If one can only practice Zen while sitting but not while standing—this would be a sickly Zen indeed; how could this become the great dharma that can save all sentient beings? Moreover, since the own-essence of the nature is not merely limited to voidness and calmness alone, if you practice that Zen which is like a senseless thing, this would not be the Zen practice that disciplines the nature but the making of a helpless invalid. Therefore, even when involved in disturbing situations, the mind should be undisturbed; even when involved with greed-creating sensory conditions, the mind should be unmoving—this is true Zen and true purity.

VII. The Main Principles of Zen

"When the six sense organs are free from activity, remove distracting thoughts and nurture the one mind. When the six sense organs are involved in activity, remove the wrong and nurture the right."

INTRODUCTION

To explain the dharma of Timeless Zen, we can make a distinction between its narrow sense and its broad sense.

In the narrow sense, it is a concept that is distinguished from seated meditation. Seated meditation is a Zen dharma that we perform while seated, whereas Timeless Zen is a Zen dharma that we perform anywhere and at any time, even as we move.

In the broad sense, Timeless Zen is a compound term that refers to Zen when we do and do not have activities, and thus is a concept that encompasses all Zen. It is a dharma of Zen that embraces not only action and rest but also walking, abiding, sitting, lying, speaking, and silence, and because Timeless Zen is a general term for the Zen dharmas performed at any time or place, all Zen dharmas ultimately converge on this dharma of Timeless Zen.

In other words, the concept of this dharma of Timeless Zen includes senses of both seated meditation and placeless Zen.

The spirit of the Timeless Zen dharma is, at its core,

about consistent practice of Zen, without being bound by concepts of time or space. This greater principle must underlie our Zen practice from the beginning.

Once this spirit has been established securely in us, we can allow no excuses for not performing Zen. There is only the mind of "Zen for this reason," "Zen for that reason," "Zen for another reason." If we have no taste for Zen, or if our will is weak, or the mind of laziness is at work, then we say that we cannot perform Zen for this reason, or for that reason, or for some other reason. We succumb to the foolishness of putting it off until later, saying that we will do it when we encounter the right opportunity, and then finishing the rest of our life without ever getting around to it.

Whatever the circumstances, then, we must start with the firm assumption that we can indeed perform Zen. We must approach it with the spirit in which we see this moment as a once-in-a-thousand-years opportunity to perform Zen and this place as the only place where we should perform Zen.

In short:
Every place is a place for Zen practice.
Every moment is a chance for Zen practice.
Every sensory condition is material for our Zen
practice.

If this spirit is not firmly established, however, we will miss out on all the good material for Zen practice. No matter how good this Zen practice material may be, it will simply slide past us without any meaning. In the process, we merely build up fearsome karmic power, layer by layer. As time passes, this karmic power snowballs; it is truly hair-raising to think what we will have to face because of it in the future.

A person who has truly understood the true meaning and methods of Zen practice, however, will be able to use every place, every moment, every sensory condition as material for Zen practice, to make steady progress over the days and months until he or she can melt away the ice-cold karmic obstacles of a thousand years, correct habits that seem ironclad, clean away the taints of many billions of years, and taste the satisfaction and ease of emancipation and freedom, the fresh and exhilarating feeling of release from a thousand years in prison.

This is why I wish to comment on the text of the "Dharma of Timeless Zen" from *The Principal Book of Won-Buddhism*: to provide a reference for companions who have embarked on Zen practice.

But because commentaries on the dharma of seated meditation have already been published and are not widely available, I will focus solely on directions for Timeless Zen and ongoing Zen.

CHAPTER ONE

COMMENTARY
ON THE TEXT

I. The Purpose of Zen

As a rule, Zen is a practice that leads to the achievement of freedom of mind by awakening to one's own nature, which is originally free from discrimination or attachment.

This section is both an explanation of the purpose of Zen practice as well as a dharma instruction that shares the broader direction of Zen.

"Discrimination" is a concept that encompasses both differentiation and discrimination. In other words, it refers to the calculations and rationale we employ when we differentiate and discriminate:

The mind that differentiates and discriminates between **grace and resentment**

The mind that differentiates and discriminates between **fondness and dislike**

The mind that differentiates and discriminates between **beauty and ugliness**

The mind that differentiates and discriminates between **good and bad**

The mind that differentiates and discriminates between **right and wrong**

The mind that differentiates and discriminates between **benefit and harm**

The mind that differentiates and discriminates between **closeness and distance**

These and all other minds that differentiate and discriminate are what we mean by discrimination.

These minds of discrimination operate necessarily through attachment.

Attachment is concept that encompasses two meanings. The first is one of resting or abiding in some place or having a mind that is captured by some place.

The second meaning is fixation. This is a state in which we have become powerfully bound and cannot escape. If we think of the first meaning as being like a criminal who has been captured, then the second meaning can be thought of as the chains that bind him. It is a state in which our freedom is already lost.

We can easily recognize states of physical bondage, but we cannot recognize the state of the mind's bondage on our own. Instead, we fall deeper and deeper into a state of more powerful bondage, all the while unaware that we are bound. This is fixation.

To sink deeply into discrimination and fixation is the foolish condition of us sentient beings who live in bondage; hell is the final destination that awaits people who live in bondage. The person engaged in Zen practice must therefore be wary of thought that discriminates and fixates.

At the root of the mind is its natural disposition. This is thus the true image of the truth enshrined within us, our allotted share within. As an entity, it is the true image of nothingness, yet being is combined with it; in this realm, all things are absent, yet it embraces all that exists.

Because this realm of the natural disposition is an entity without the sort of discrimination and fixation described earlier, its true image is one where emancipation or even freedom has no separate meaning.

"Awakening" means both realizing and attaining. In other words, we achieve awakening and thus reach a state of recovery, of restoration. We have found our fundamental nature, which had been forgotten and lost from all the defilements of discrimination and fixation, and we have once again claimed it. Awakening encompasses both finding and understanding, as well as discovering and claiming.

We human beings possess a physical body, and from it emerge various signs—clusters of the mind—identifying the "self." Out of this surges a torrent of selfish motives and delusions, their numbers beyond our ability to count. Combine these with the instinctive urges of the physical body, and our minds truly are a sight to see with their thousand forms and myriad of signs.

So it is that the realm of our true nature becomes tainted as can be, tattered and torn, weak and helpless.

It is much like when some foreign substance becomes mixed with and contaminates water that was originally pure. Once contaminated, the water loses its original life force; it may even become toxic, causing damage by threatening life wherever it goes. But once we purify that water, restore it to the way it was originally, the life force of the water not only returns; it again functions as grace, bringing life to all things wherever it goes.

This is how the realm of our true nature is. Originally, it existed without discrimination or fixation, but as we have lived our life in our physical body, various discriminations and fixations have arisen and sapped our true nature of its life force.

In our lives, then, it is desperately important for us to reclaim this lost realm of our true nature. We can also turn this around to mean that we are recovering our lost freedom, or achieving liberation from all bondage.

There are two ways in which people tend to live their

lives in bondage.

The first is external bondage, and the second is internal bondage. External bondage refers to a state of actually, physically being bound. Internal bondage refers to the inward state where our mind is powerfully bound to something. Both types of bondage, external and internal, mean that we have already lost our freedom; our range of motion is restricted to the minimum, and any hope of enjoying a vast world is utterly ignored.

But while external bondage means only that we are physically unfree, internal bondage means that we lose all freedom of body and mind, so the torment is far greater. With physical bondage, there is little risk that we will transgress because we do not have the freedom to act. With mental bondage, we are not subject to physical constraints and so we may be incited by the minions of Māra to commit transgressions with absolute power. It is a truly dangerous state in which to be.

Once we are in this state, none of our possessions— our body, our mind—are truly ours. All are subordinate to the king of the Māras. It is for this reason that the spirit and purpose of Zen are to seek freedom of the mind by gaining awakening to the fundamental nature that is free of discrimination and fixation.

We often speak of "Zen practice," "mind practice,"

or "meditation practice." There are various methods of practice and cultivation in which the mind is our material. Those methods may be too numerous for us to count, but all of them are ways to discipline our basic nature. Yet such practice without the definite goal of disciplining our true nature can lead us to stray onto errant paths. It can send us sliding into the mire of unbalanced practice and block the path to limitless growth. We can succumb to fearsome, perverted views and commit transgressions that are more fearsome still. The practitioner must therefore proceed on the firm understanding that he or she is disciplining his or her fundamental nature.

From the standpoint of all things in the universe, the fundamental nature is the origin; from the standpoint of truth, it is the true image; from the standpoint of us people, it is our original nature; and from the standpoint of the Buddha, it is the buddha nature. Thus the origin, the true image, the original nature, and the buddha nature are all one and undivided.

It is similar to the way the water in the sea, the water in the earth, the water in plants, and the water in an animal's body are all the same moisture. The role and functions of that moisture may change with the vessel that contains it, but in all cases it behaves according to the properties of water.

We can also rephrase this to say that the water's role and functions may change according to the reality that it faces, but in no case does it deviate from the properties that water possesses.

We can apply the same analogy to the role of the fundamental nature. It differs according to perspective— the origin of all things that exist, the true image of the truth, the original nature of a person, and the buddha nature of the Buddha—and so it may appear to us to have different roles or aspects in each case, but the true image in all of these does not deviate from the properties of the *Il-Won-Sang* truth.

As we see here, the fundamental nature is something so obvious, so definite, yet it is also a void concept, such that when we look inside in search of a true image, there is nothing that we can grasp, nothing that we can hold on to. There is nothing that it shows us, nothing that it gives us to hear or understand.

Yet this void true image contains within it every single thing in existence. It reflects all phenomena hidden and visible, without fail. In every situation, it offers the appropriate functioning for that situation, without the slightest error. What could we possibly say to express its mystery, its immensity, its accuracy, its utter exquisiteness? I have sought to teach it with a *hwadu*, or a keyword—

the nut pine before the garden, for example—but this too was in vain.

In truth, no explanation of this realm could fully express the fundamental nature. The true image is such that the more one explains, the farther it recedes; what, then, can we possibly do? It is truly an impossible task.

But recent developments in civilization have given a richer store of materials with which to compare it. Developments in linguistics have given a richer range of plausible explanations. It has become far easier than ever before for a person of quick wit and depth of vision to detect.

The practitioner should therefore awaken first to this realm of the true nature. Only then can he or she attain the skill to discipline it.

There is an old saying about this: "Practice before awakening is not true practice; practice after awakening is true practice." It is the same principle by which we must understand the properties of a car before we can drive the car correctly.

It cannot be the same, then, when a practitioner enters into practice with an understanding of his or her true nature and when he or she does so without such an understanding. If we enter without knowing what our fundamental nature is, we may fall into traps from time to time, or roam about on errant paths.

For this reason, we must have a correct understanding of our fundamental nature. It is not something rigid, nor is it something confined to any framework. We may call it the true image of purity and quiescence, but as the need arises, our nature also commands, and commands frankly, the autumn wildfire blazing through our six sense organs at every moment.

This is why we must balance our discipline of our nature between discipline in times of action and discipline in times of rest, nurturing the skill to use the mind well and according to our will in any situation. If our every action in every situation manifests a practice in accordance with the self-nature, then we have ascended to the lotus pedestal of the unequaled rank.

Awakening to the self-nature and achieving freedom of the mind is thus the core and the goal of Zen practice.

Since time immemorial, those who have been determined to achieve the great Way have all practiced Zen.

This is a reference to the past of Zen practice. It presents to us the way forward for all people who seek the Way.

Since long ago, people were often said to have worried that when few people were practicing Zen in a country's meditation halls, it meant that the nation's talents would soon be exhausted. This expressed the difficulty that awaits anyone with ambitions of achieving the Way, or anything great, without first attaining the powers of Zen. Even in the absence of any consciousness of Zen in itself, those who apply the great power of aspiration, or who concentrate on a problem to be solved as a *hwadu*, will ultimately create outcomes of great achievement through the functioning of that Zen power.

The message of this passage is thus that anyone who aspires to the great Way or great achievement should first build his or her mental strength with Zen.

It is a powerful message: To succeed in his or her practice, the practitioner should first engage in Zen practice.

II. The Dharma of Mahāyāna Meditation

If people intend to practice genuine Zen, they first should take true voidness as the substance and marvelous existence as the function . . .

This passage states the premise that Zen practice must be based on the principle of true voidness and the principle of marvelous existence. Before we proceed, we should have a definite understanding of the meanings of "true voidness" and "marvelous existence," for this is an essential question that we must apply to our Zen practice.

True voidness is truly void because it is the true image of the fundamental nature of all phenomena, which is utterly empty, wholly empty, thoroughly empty. If so much as a hair were to impinge on it, it would not be the pure true image of that fundamental nature. This is the realm in which our mind is rooted. While all trees and grasses may live rooted in the ground, we creatures of numinous nature live rooted in the void. This realm is the realm of true voidness and the hometown of all things in creation.

Because of this, we must base our mind on the realm of true voidness. However much the outside sensory conditions may roil, our inner mind must be able to live in peace in the true voidness if we are to take true voidness as its substance. If we do not establish substance in the true void, it will become contaminated, disturbed, foolish, and wrong.

By marvelous existence, we mean that while the realm of the fundamental nature is merely void and calm, it is not something confined merely to nothingness. We mean that from time to time and from place to place, it is accompanied by creative transformations and change. This is why we speak of true voidness and marvelous existence. Indeed, because it is marvelous existence amid true voidness and true voidness amid marvelous existence, there remains not a trace of absence when we view it in terms of the void, yet when we view it in terms of marvelous existence, it manifests constant, omnipotent creative transformations.

Thus, we are speaking of practice that is based in true voidness, yet builds our power to manifest the function of marvelous existence. To put it more simply, it is the mind in which we clear away all the noncharacter elements and infinitely nurture the elements of character. This is what we refer to as "the livelihood of the mind." It explains why the livelihood of buddhas is said to be so unfathomably great that they can use it and use it and never exhaust it. In short, Zen practice is about ridding ourselves of all that must be abandoned, and possessing all that must be possessed.

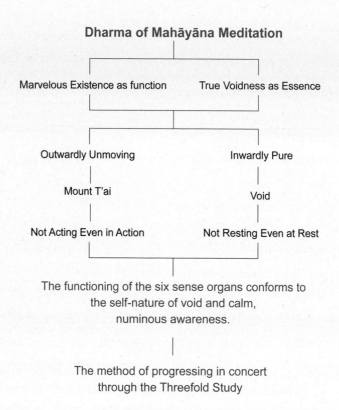

Dharma of Mahāyāna Meditation

Marvelous Existence as function   True Voidness as Essence

Outwardly Unmoving   Inwardly Pure

Mount T'ai   Void

Not Acting Even in Action   Not Resting Even at Rest

The functioning of the six sense organs conforms to
the self-nature of void and calm,
numinous awareness.

The method of progressing in concert
through the Threefold Study

———

. . . and, externally, be unmoving like Mount T'ai when in contact with the myriad of sensory conditions, and, internally, keep the mind unsullied, like empty space.

———

This dharma instruction states for us the core principles of responding through the dharma of Timeless Zen both externally and internally. For most practitioners, the core question is how to respond to the sensory conditions and hindrances of Māra that infiltrate from outside, and how to respond to the defilements and hindrances of Māra that emerge inside. That is what this passage captures so definitively.

All people live their lives being faced with sensory conditions, both adverse and favorable. The question, then, is how our mind functions under the influence of those conditions: Does it function as a storm, function as a moderate wind, function as a light breeze, or function without any wind at all? Just as the peak of Mount T'ai remains unmoved through any typhoon, so the unmoved mind, the mind like Mount T'ai, is one that is maintained without the slightest shaking even when it is buffeted by the typhoon of adverse and favorable sensory conditions, the conditions of the five desires and three poisons.

All of us live a life in which our thoughts follow an inward cycle of repetition: rising like the grass in the field, then disappearing, vanishing, only to rise again. No weed can grow in ground that is dead. It must be living ground if any grass or trees are to sprout and grow. The more fertile the ground, the lusher the plants grow. The constant emergence of delusions in a person's mind is evidence that he or she has a living mind. But if the farmer's sincere tending of this earth leaves no space for weeds to set root, if we sow and grow the five grains and hundred fruits, the field will be a field of gold. So it is with our mind. When we give no space for all the defilements to grow, when we produce only wisdom, the world of the mind will be filled with jewels beyond price.

It is for this reason that we should keep the mind like the void, and never lose its purity. All weeds are easiest to tend to when we pull them out before they have a chance to thicken; recognizing and tending to all our defilements when they first arise, before they progress into fearsome karmic obstacles, is both the easiest way and the wisest. Once weeds have been neglected and left to grow profuse, removing them becomes a very strenuous endeavor. Defilements also become like unbridled ponies when left neglected; you never know whose grain field they will ruin.

Furthermore, once clusters of karmic power have

formed, all the self-power and other-power that we can muster may not be enough to extricate us.

Foolish as we are, we sentient beings do not recognize how very fearsome karmic obstacles are. Trapped by these powerful barriers, we are not ourselves. We become puppets of the king of the Māras, and we do not hesitate to commit fearsome transgressions and unwholesomeness. How can we hope to withstand the anguish?

This Zen practice, then, is an effort to extinguish those fearsome karmic obstacles.

Let the mind function so that it is not acting even in action and not resting even at rest.

The meaning of this dharma instruction is that we should not fixate on action when we were acting, nor fixate on rest when we are resting. The essence of it is that we should have the resting state of mind when in action, and the acting state of mind when at rest. To put it in more practical terms, "action" refers to times of movement, and movement refers to the actions of our eyes and ears and nose and mouth and body and mind as they encounter colors, sounds, smells, tastes, physical contact, and thoughts. In other words, it is the state of the six sense organs functioning as they encounter the sensory conditions of the six sense objects. The sensory conditions of the six sense objects, in turn, can be rephrased as all sensory conditions, both favorable and adverse.

When we face these favorable and adverse sensory conditions yet are not buried by them, we may act, yet we are without action. We encounter favorable conditions without being buried in favorable conditions; we encounter adverse conditions without being buried in adverse conditions. All sensory conditions are only briefly passing clouds, not lingering true images. This is what is meant by not being rolled about by sounds and colors, not being drawn into defilement by favorable or adverse sensory conditions.

So although the six sense organs may be blazing like an autumn wildfire, the proper approach (right essence) for the world of the mind is the way that is ever just as it is.

"Rest" refers to the times when we are not moving, the times when we need not move, the times when we do not have to move. These are the times when we let go entirely of the original mind, or when countless defilements pour forth from the karmic obstacles that we typically encounter. "The small person is incapable of doing nothing when he is at leisure," it is said, and it is indeed no easy matter to avoid becoming separated from this mind of the Way. That is why we have long been told to "be cautious when we are alone." The person who truly has the power not to lose the mind of the Way when he or she is alone can truly be said to be a person of the Way.

The words about being "not resting even while at rest" are thus an admonition to preserve the mind of the Way as something vivid and alive even when we are at rest—to be thorough about the work of fostering the mind of the Way. Not resting while at rest is a matter of ceaselessly doing the work of replenishing all the energies of the mind of the Way: fostering the original energy, fostering the true energy, fostering the night energy, fostering the right energy. When this happens, our times of rest are times of working to produce wisdom, and our times of action are times of working to use that wisdom to manifest merits. In so doing, we accord with the self-nature in both action and rest—what is referred to as "the self-nature without division in action and rest."

The greatest *hwadu*s for a person cultivating the Way have to do with the functioning of the mind. Where to have the mind abide, how to preserve it, how to use it— once we have grasped the reasons from this, we are said to have grasped the path of practice. Unless we do this, we are still in a state of wandering.

If we do so, then there will be no discrimination that is separate from purity, so that the functioning of the six sense organs will accord with the self-nature of the void and calm, numinous awareness.

So long as a person has a physical body, he or she cannot avoid encountering sensory conditions: seeing, hearing, smelling, tasting, touching, and thinking. If these contradictions enter us through the six sense organs as we encounter them, we are bound to experience all sorts of feelings and impressions. As we encounter those feelings and impressions, we produce still other imaginings, truly building and tearing down the world systems of the trichiliocosm. In the process, fearsome new karmic consciousness takes shape, and that karmic consciousness functions as a binding force that ensnares us once again. This is the law of the five aggregates: form, sensation, perception, mental formations, and consciousness.

When we speak of "no discrimination that is separate from purity," this refers to the original mind of the mind world that is just as it is naturally, that remains not the slightest bit shaken or tainted even when buffeted by a veritable typhoon of favorable or adverse sensory conditions. No matter what terrible thunder or lighting or storm or winds may come upon the void, that void is always just as it is and intact; when they pass, not a trace is left behind.

Though we may encounter sensory conditions as need arises, and though the actions of the six sense organs may blaze like an autumn wildfire, the original mind remains just as it is, and after the conditions have passed there is not a trace of them left behind. It is as clean and pure as if nothing ever happened.

Yet the void and calm, numinous awareness of the self-nature remains undeluded, responding to all sensory conditions with moderation, in accordance with regulation, and without constraint, free from bias or reliance, excessiveness, or deficiency. In this case, we speak of a state where the functions of the six sense organs are in accordance with the self-nature of void and calm, numinous awareness.

Because this is a dharma of cultivation for all weather and all directions, it is called the "Dharma of Mahāyāna meditation." It is a dharma for practice in which we can be guaranteed effects and results in the three great powers, and it should properly be performed in concert with the Threefold Study.

III. When and Where We Can Practice Zen

Give rise to a mind that, even while responding, does not abide anywhere.

This dharma instruction comes from the Diamond Sutra. We can understand it to mean that we should "produce the mind that is without fixation anywhere, even as we respond to all external sensory conditions." In other words, we should respond to all objects, but without abiding in any one place. We do not fixate on wealth, sex, fame, or gain; the concept of the ego, the four apparent forms, or any apparent phenomena at all; or the aspect of the dharma, or on the aspect of that which is not dharma.

When we produce a mind while fixating, it is like the passage of light through tinted glasses. With those glasses, we cannot immediately see what comes in and goes out. It appears inverted, distorted, and we develop various incorrect views, including overstatement, understatement, exaggeration, disguise, and embellishment.

Fixation is thus the main offender when our wisdom is buried. We have a fixation, and our wisdom cannot become clear—never mind achieving liberation or freedom. This is why every scripture of Buddhism warns first and foremost to be wary of fixation.

This is precisely the great dharma of practice that remains unmoved amid the myriad of sensory conditions.

This is not a dharma of remaining unmoved when no sensory conditions are present. One who flees sensory conditions so as not to be moved is one who has lost already.

One often finds people who have taken a liking to Zen, who have decided to give it a try, and so they look about in search of somewhere quiet, where no one is present. Worse still, they might give up their livelihood or simply seek out some tunnel, without any thought for their family or their obligations to society and country. All they are doing is making themselves more powerless. How unfortunate our eternal lives will be when we have not created blessings because we have shunned all our duties!

Moreover, sensory conditions are an important source of material for practitioners in their practice. This material belongs to the person who uses it; it functions as income for its user. To flee this material is to be as foolish as a person who wishes to swim yet flees the water or a person who wishes to drive yet shuns the highway.

Even if we have suffered some harm or hurt amid our sensory conditions, this too serves as a greater income and awakening. Ultimately, we will achieve great powers from these conditions, so we may be buried in sensory conditions of wealth, sex, fame, or gain yet remain unmoved by them; we can live amid the storm of favorable and adverse sensory conditions yet remain unmoved by that storm. This dharma of practice is what we call the great dharma, the dharma of Mahāyāna meditation.

———————

This dharma may seem extremely difficult, but if we come to understand in detail the methods of practice, then even a farmer wielding a hoe can practice Zen, as can a carpenter wielding a hammer, a clerk using an abacus, and an official seeing to an administrative matter; and we can practice Zen even while going about or staying at home.

———————

This passage stresses that while the dharma of practice that I have discussed so far may seem impossibly difficult to someone without a taste for Zen or who merely sees it as hard, anyone who understands in detail the method of cultivation will be able to practice Zen, and he or she can practice it while doing anything at all. In other words, we can practice Zen in action, while working, while making a livelihood with any kind of profession, and we can be assured of its results.

This dharma instruction also means that we should not merely view Zen as difficult and that we should not be bound by time or place, by action or rest, or by profession. In this way, it motivates us to practice Zen. It teaches us that we must first find the method of Zen practice.

What need is there to bother with choosing a specific place and with talking about action or rest?

This message once again highlights the mistaken views on the methods of Zen practice that were described before.

How sad it is when someone who wishes to practice Zen wanders about in search of a "good place to practice Zen" or who wishes to stop all activity and sit quietly when he or she practices, for such a person has succumbed to the foolishness of failing to make effective use of time and material for Zen practice, to take the opportunity to build Zen powers steadily over the days and months. He or she will miss out on all the priceless gems and even on those areas that have been disciplined amid sensory conditions. Moreover, however well we may practice Zen alone in a quiet environment, it will become very difficult for us to sustain that successful Zen mind when the place changes and the time is different. This is called the "sickly Zen," where we merely sit, and cannot practice when standing.

Anyone who wishes to practice Zen is therefore urged to abandon any thoughts of distinctions of space or distinctions of action and rest and to adopt instead an attitude of seeking Zen practice consistently, in every place, at every time.

IV. The Reality of Zen

However, for people who are first beginning to practice Zen, the mind is not easily controlled according to their wishes; it is like training an ox where, if the reins of the mind are dropped even for a moment, it will instantly harm one's commitment to the Way.

This passage truly hits on the key point about which a beginning Zen practitioner should be wary. After all the reading, reading, and more reading; after the reciting, reciting, and more reciting; after putting everything completely in our head, it is the thing that we should carry with us like a *hwadu* at all places and at all times and never again let it go, for here lies a method, a path, a light, and a hope.

The reference here is to those who are first beginning to practice Zen. The truth, however, is that the mind does not perform as we wish it to even when we have practiced Zen for a considerable amount of time. We want to hold our mind firm, yet it not only eludes our grasp but comes and goes, racing hither and thither, appearing and disappearing—it truly is a sight to behold. The passage makes an analogy here to an ox: Born as a calf, it suckles on its mother's milk, and as it grows and its legs become powerful, it races busily, coming and going. It is the very picture of freedom, without regard for time or place. It is utterly without constraint. This is how we sentient beings are when our defilements behave rashly and willfully as karma dictates.

At this point, the ox's master makes up his mind to bind the ox and bring it in line. He first pierces a hole in the ox's nose to install a ring; then he attaches the bridle so that he can pull the ox from behind by drawing on the reins. Once he has taken these steps, even the wildest ox or pony cannot move about. Eventually, it will be tamed.

As much as the ox may race about at first, eventually it will not be able to withstand the ever more powerful tugging, and it will finally become docile. Here we find a skillful means of taming the wild sentient-being mind.

Each of us has within our mind a wild "mind ox" that needs taming. We have the master mind (teacher) who seeks to tame it, and we have the mind bridle (the dharma reins) connecting between. This passage tells us to find it, uncover it fully, and use it appropriately.

The original intent of Zen lies in taming the dangerous and mistaken mind into a mind that will create only blessings. To put it more simply, it means taming the wild sentient-being mind that would shatter ultimate bliss and create only hell, and turning it into a buddha-bodhisattva mind that will shatter hell and create only ultimate bliss.

If we wish to embark on this endeavor, there are three essential materials that we must have first: an object in need of taming (the wild sentient-being mind), a master to supervise it (the pledge), and a bridle and reins connecting them (the dharma reins). Taming the mind without using these three materials is impossible. We must start by making certain that these three are present.

After that, we must hold on tight to the dharma reins and not let go whenever the sentient-being mind rages. As we keep hold on the reins, the raging sentient-being mind is caught by them. It suffers harsher and harsher constraints the more fiercely it rages. The pain is greater when our karmic obstacles are great, but if we merely hold on to the dharma reins and do not let go, the mind will finally be tamed.

But one moment of inattention, one release of the dharma reins, and the sentient-being mind will rage more fiercely than before. It is now like the pony that is freed from the bridle. We must therefore make sure never to let go of the reins before the mind is fully tamed.

We must be very wary here about any irresponsible inattention from the master who is trying to tame the mind. A momentary lapse can tear down the most painstakingly built of houses. Once it has collapsed, we have no recourse but to start building it all over again. At times, we may even have to endure retribution for the harm we have caused to those around us.

We must therefore be very cautious about any lapses by the master.

Therefore, if you keep exerting yourself without letting go of that spirit which is ready to fight to the bitter end, no matter how alluring the sensory conditions you face may be, the mind will gradually become tamed and you will reach a state where the mind will do what you wish.

As hard as we may work to not allow any lapses, we may find ourselves faced with instinctive desires or fearsome karmic power, and we feel that we absolutely cannot defeat them, that no other effective solutions exist. And so we grow tired, we feel no pleasure, we feel that we are not "cut out" for practice, we feel bothered, and the retreating mind emerges. We simply give up. At this point, we may be drawn to become the sport of the minions of Māra, and feel worse and more scattered than before we ever started our practice. Our morale drops, our will hits rock bottom, our physical energy sags like never before, and we succumb to deep worry, the feeling that we can never escape these sensory conditions.

The message here is that when we face moments like this, we should have courage and stay strong, without ever letting go of our fighting spirit.

Even the minions of Māra do not have the strength

to keep raging endlessly. There comes a time when the minions of Māra too have reached the height of their raging and their strength must wane.

The willingness to wait for this moment and to seize power again—is the spirit of readiness to fight to the bitter end. We can seize the initiative at these moments. It is said that success and failure are both parts of a day's work for a soldier; so too is it characteristic for someone cultivating the Way to experience victories and defeats, over and over, in his or her fight with sensory conditions. We simply cannot become complacent over a single victory, nor should we resign ourselves after a single defeat. If we have lost ninety-nine times, a victory in the final match is all that we need to be a winner.

Through this process, through all the twists and turns, strength will build up in our minds, and the power of the minions of Māra will gradually fade. We will reach the stage where the mind ox is tamed and the master has gained dominance and can command it at will. This is what we mean by reaching "a state where the mind will do what you wish."

Each and every time you are in contact with a sensory condition, do not forget to keep the thought in mind that an opportunity for practice has arrived, always taking a suitable measure of whether or not you are affected by that sensory condition.

The key to understanding this dharma instruction is to take particular heed of the words "do not forget to keep the thought in mind."

As long as people are surviving in this world, they are in contact with sensory conditions of one form or another. They experience all sorts of feelings of joy or sadness as these conditions dictate. Now, it is all well and good to experience feelings, but over time we find ourselves becoming buried in the sensory conditions, and by the time we are buried, our freedom has already disappeared. The phenomena of life make it a struggle to extricate ourselves from this phenomenon of burial. At times, we do even possess the mind to try to break free.

Rather than merely allowing ourselves to be whisked away by those sensory conditions, our first thought (what we should keep in mind) when those conditions arise should be, "This is a time to practice. A time to practice has come around." After that, we are told to check to see whether we are being drawn to those conditions or not.

In other words, we should respond to these moments by looking objectively at what is inside our mind.

The mind without practice tends to respond unthinkingly with a reflexive show of emotion when it encounters a sensory condition; it questions the right or wrong of it, the good or bad; it spontaneously rejects or covets, so that we cannot make a profound choice in our action. And so the waves of disturbance, delusion, and wrongdoing are never-ending.

This is the phenomenon of being drawn by sensory conditions, of sinking into sensory conditions. The further we sink, the more the master who should be supporting our right self loses strength, finally succumbing instead to bondage.

This passage gives us a method for responding before we sink too far and succumb to bondage.

When sensory conditions arrive, we should first think, "The time to practice has come," and look closely to see if we are being drawn or not. To fully see when we are being drawn and not drawn, without missing a thought—this is how we measure our level of mindfulness. Letting go of checking this for even a moment is unmindfulness. Once the mind's habit of measuring its level of mindfulness in every circumstance has taken root, we will naturally understand that every sensory condition is a time to practice, and the mind's alertness to whether we are being drawn or not will become firmly established of its own accord.

When we reach the stage where the mind almost completely takes care of itself, the mind's tendency to be drawn will be fully resolved, and the mind's ability to not be drawn will gain resolute strength. There may be times, however, when our longstanding karmic power or habits make it very difficult to control how we are drawn from one situation to the next. No sooner do we fight one thing off than another ambushes us, and it is unclear whether there will ever come a day when we reach that refuge where we are not drawn.

At moments like this, we need a trick. There are times when we cannot fight something head on because our adversary is too fierce and strong and we are too weak. When this happens, a better approach than a frontal assault is to gently guide that wildly powerful raging attention elsewhere so that it disappears on its own. The easiest way is to recite the buddha's name with concentrated focus, but at times we may be able to easily control and quiet that wild, powerful raging by directing it elsewhere—by working with, watching, or listening to something of interest. That is the trick.

When we make it our business to go after something head on when it is too strong and fierce, not only will we never win but we will suffer occupation by it when we lose in the end. As a result, we may endure much suffering of the mind; our mind and body may grow tired, so that we abandon everything and sink into a mire of resignation. A frontal assault should not be our first course of action. When we are certain that our adversary is similar in strength to us, or that we are stronger, then we should by all means tackle it head on and fight to the end. Before we do that, though, we need a suitable tool, a trick that will allow us a stealthy escape. From there, we can build our strength and try the fight again.

———————

Thus, once there is a gradual increase in instances of behavior in which the mind does what you wish, you may from time to time let yourself be put in situations that you normally would find extremely attractive or abhorrent. If the mind is moved as before, then your commitment to the Way is immature; but if it is unmoved, then you will know that this is proof that your commitment to the Way is ripening.

———————

This passage explains the next steps that follow from the aforementioned measuring of mindfulness.

When we are fighting against sensory conditions, we can easily overcome them by mobilizing great zeal with a faithful mind, a vow, exertion, and the accumulation of merits, but doing so when the mind is frayed can be very difficult and sometimes impossible. The trick at these moments is to tell the truth to our teacher and our friends in the dharma. By drawing on both self-power and other-power, we can easily pass through. The more we try to conceal the problem, out of unnecessary shame and foolish pride, the stronger the minions of Māra grow and the more we weaken in comparison, raising the odds that we will suffer a defeat.

As we check whether we are being drawn or not in our mind, we must fight a life-or-death battle: Will it be the minions of Māra who win, or will it be the dharma? Only when we keep that fighting spirit until the bitter end will the minions of Māra finally weaken and the dharma grow strong, and ultimately there will be an increase in the number of instances when we act according to our own will. The step that we must take, without missing these opportunities, is to ensure that we encounter sensory conditions. In short, we take on the sensory conditions of the things that we profoundly like and profoundly dislike in our lives.

This is a matter of *slightly* taking them on; we must not adopt an attitude of giving in fully. If we give in a little bit and sense that we cannot handle it, then we need to pull back again and stay far away. Otherwise, we may create an outcome where we are miserably defeated.

When we practice this cycle of giving in to sensory conditions and backing away, testing the waters and disciplining ourselves, we gradually build strength in our mind, while the power of Māra weakens, allowing us to seize the initiative for a hundred victories in a hundred battles. Only then can we rest easy. We must be wary of ever letting go of the mind that checks whether we are being drawn, for it can become a limitation that hinders further development or cause us to fall farther.

However, at the very time that you realize that the mind is unmoving, do not let down your guard, for it is unmoving through your employing the mental powers, rather than naturally unmoving. The mind has been well tamed only when it is unmoving even if left unguarded.

As this shows, we gradually develop over the course of exerting ourselves with Zen practice, and at times we use the mind as we want to. It may seem impossible at first that we could ever use our mind as we wish, but when we emerge from the deep tunnel, there are more and more instances in which, having made these efforts, we can now use our mind as we want to. If we continue making efforts without allowing any lapses, then we will gradually develop until the number of instances when we do as we wish will reach about half. When we apply ourselves with even greater effort, the number of victories rises further, and if we continue exerting and accumulating merits without letting go of the reins, we finally reach the stage of a hundred victories in a hundred battles. Even at the stage of a hundred victories in a hundred battles, however, the war is not completely over. There are gangs that lurk in wait to try again at the next opportunity, and this means that we cannot let our guard down for a moment.

As we gradually become tamed, and the fiercely raging gang slowly disappears, we can practice loosening those tightly pulled reins a bit and seizing them again, and then letting go. We will find that we are not drawn by sensory conditions—that no matter what conditions come, favorable or adverse, the five desires, or any other conditions, we respond with only serenity and not the slightest disturbance. At this point, we truly have cleared away the karma of a thousand years; we have shed the chains of ten thousand years. How exhilarating it is! What words could express that feeling of freedom and liberation? This is truly the moment when we recover our original image and restore our sovereignty.

So only when we are clearly conscious that our goal is the realm of the mind that is unmoving even if left unguarded, our direction will be clear, and we will not wander on errant paths.

V. The Results of Zen Practice

If you continue for a long time practicing Zen so as to put an end to all the defilements and achieve freedom of mind, then you will be centered like an iron pillar and defended from the outside like a stone wall, so that neither wealth nor status nor honor nor glory can coax the mind, nor can anyone use weapons or authority to make the mind submit.

Among the many endeavors that people engage in as they live their lives, there are some for which everything is decided at once, but usually they are resolved only through effort over a long time. Some things may be resolved in one fell swoop, but even in such cases, that final resolution was actually brought about by thorough investigation and preparation.

This Zen practice is also something that does not happen all at once. The effects of Zen and its might are ensured through long periods of effort. If our karmic power is light, it may happen relatively easily; if our karmic power is dense, it will take some difficulty and require more commitment and time.

The strange thing, though, is that many people are unwilling to make the effort; they simply want the characteristics of the outcome. An old saying puts it this way: "Though we may seek achievement within, we cannot attain it through desire alone." This is all the more true for Zen practice.

It is through long and continued effort at severing our defilements and integrating the mind by repeating this process over and over that the power of those defilements weakens and the power of the controller who establishes that integrated mind gradually builds, until we finally bring all of the defilements into submission.

It is because the crowds that obstruct the integrated mind vanish that the controllers regain freedom. That freedom is something no one can obstruct, something no one can get in the way of. No matter how the sensory conditions may rage as they come in from outside, we remain unshaken like Mount T'ai; the analogy is of a rock wall that remains unmoved even when it is being buffeted by ten million sensory conditions. At this point, riches and honor present no temptation, nor do weapons or power pose any threat.

Ordinary people, when given rights and authority, become avaricious and unconcerned with decorum, shame, or a sense of face. When faced with threats of weapons or power, not only do they wave the white flag but they are incited to do things that would otherwise be unimaginable. Where there is profit, there is right; where there is none, there is wrong.

Having determined the places in which the weapons and power are right and those where they are wrong, the latter slip away from our attention. Our standards for judging right and wrong are interests and harm rather than good and bad, or justice and iniquity.

What will come of the world when our standards for believing and not believing are based on weapons or authority rather than on fact and reason? Indeed, if this is the level of our consciousness, the ideals of democracy are but a vain dream.

If this society is truly to flower with the ideals of

democracy, then each of its members must perform Zen, using that power to develop a mature civic consciousness: a mind that is not appeased by riches or honor, a mind that does not bend before weapons or power. Once we have done this, the ideals of democracy will burst into brilliant flowers, and each one of us will rejoice in the truest freedom.

Practicing all dharmas in this manner, you will never be enticed or obstructed, and even while residing in this dusty world, you will constantly attain hundreds and thousands of samādhis.

"All dharmas" here refers to the doctrines of *Won-Buddhism*, the order's constitution. It encompasses all the norms and the positive law operating in society, all the scriptures in the religious order, and all the ways of ethics and the principles of the world.

We can divide all dharmas into two types by their character: dharmas of prohibition (the things we must not do) and dharmas of rightfulness (the things we ought to do). Dharmas of prohibition are like precepts that we must not break; dharmas of rightfulness are like norms we must uphold.

As we practice all of these terms, we encounter no enticements or obstructions. There are no gangs that prevent us, nor meddlers who stand in our way.

How many times does it happen that there is one corner of our mind that wishes to do what is right, yet we cannot because we are enticed by wealth, sex, fame, or gain? We cannot because we are enticed by indolence. We cannot because we are obstructed by greed. We cannot because we are hung up on closeness and distance. We cannot because we are obstructed by the distinction between "ourselves" and "others." There is a song that expresses this state of mind well. "Why did I do it / knowing that I ought not to / Why did I do it / knowing that I ought not to," the lyrics say. We do drugs, knowing that we ought not to. We drink too much, knowing that we ought not to do. We know what is right, yet we cannot do it. We know what is wrong, yet do it anyway. This phenomenon shows us the rock bottom of our spiritual strength.

But once we have gained the power of Zen, no minions of Māra can stand before us as we go about practicing all the dharmas. Indeed, all our thoughts and all our family are mobilized for the thing that we are doing. There is no one and nothing that can stand in the way of it.

In this way, we are free and autonomous, without any enticements or obstructions in all the dharmas. Both dharmas of prohibition and dharmas of rightfulness translate into practice with one mind. We have no hesitation, no vacillation, no crowds that obstruct or hinder us.

Instead, we focus the mind on each of our affairs, whatever we happen to be doing, and use these as material to practice all dharmas, so that even when we are faced with the "dusty world," we are said to attain "hundreds and thousands of samādhis." Hundreds and thousands of samādhis refers to the state in which the mind is focused only on practicing wisdom.

As we continue focusing the mind on each and every affair that we engage in, that focused mind eventually reaches a deep place where we arrive at the stage of selflessness. This is called "selflessness of the one mind." This stage of selflessness is the realm of samādhi, and it is hundreds and thousands of samādhis because we reach the summit of the one mind in every affair.

At this point, our affairs succeed, our capabilities are honed as we build them, and we reach the realm of freedom and autonomy no matter what confronts us. It is a world of ecstasy that we can truly only imagine.

Once you reach this stage, the entire world will be transformed into the one genuine realm of reality, and right and wrong, good and evil, and all the defiled and pure dharmas will become the single taste of ghee.

"This stage" refers to the aforementioned stage in which we can enter samādhi in any circumstance—where we can achieve hundreds and thousands of samādhis. Because the entire world is used as one genuine realm of reality, wisdom is produced in every place. The dharma is produced, grace is produced, and paradise is built.

"The entire world" speaks of a phenomenon whereby right and wrong, good and evil, exist in confusion, and where clean and dirty are all knotted together. Thus, we produce wisdom even amid right and wrong; we reap wisdom even amid good and bad; and we discover and claim wisdom even amid dirt and cleanliness. What words exist to describe the solid, satisfied feeling that we encounter at every moment? The term that is used is "the single taste of ghee"—the greatest flavor, produced by the greatest clarification of butter. It is the feeling of having experienced the best taste in this world.

A top chef can make a brilliant meal out of any

ingredients in the world. Once the power of Zen reaches its pinnacle, we can produce wisdom, produce the dharma, and build a paradise of this world in any situation. In this way, the power of Zen is the omnipotent wish-fulfilling gem that makes anything possible.

This state is called the gateway of nonduality. Freedom in birth and death, liberation from the cycle of rebirths, and the ultimate bliss of the pure land all emerge through this gateway.

"This" refers to the state described before, in which we have attained the power to realize the single taste of ghee in any situation.

The "gateway of nonduality" means the gate that does not divide inside from outside; it is the gate by which we enter a world where the discriminations of all objective concepts have ceased. Good and bad, then, are not separate; right and wrong are not separate; dirty and clean are not separate; like and dislike are not separate; distant and close are not separate; favorable and adverse are not separate. All discriminating concepts disappear and there is no enticement or obstruction anywhere, with equality of good or bad, equality of right and wrong, equality of dirty and clean, equality of like and dislike, equality of far and near, equality of favorable and adverse.

We have entered the world of equality, where there is no wind or waves of disturbance and delusion and wrongdoing in the self-nature—the world of the gateway of nonduality.

It is thus samādhi in wholesome sensory conditions, samādhi in unwholesome sensory conditions, samādhi in right sensory conditions, samādhi in wrong sensory conditions. The objects that entice and obstruct and pull and block in dirty and clean, like and dislike, far and near, favorable and adverse—in any circumstances at all—are all wiped away so that everywhere there is freedom and liberation and ultimate bliss.

It is freedom because the things that we cannot do because our life obstructs us have disappeared; there is nothing we cannot do because we fear death. It is liberation because the chains of karma do not bind us; it is the pure land because the mind-ground is clean and pure and undefiled. And what is the pleasure of the dharma realm that transcends suffering and happiness if not ultimate bliss? All of these things, the passage tells us, are the world that we must pass through—the gateway of nonduality—to attain. The message is that we must praise and admire the results achieved through Zen practice, and arouse our minds to practice Zen.

VI. Prejudices Regarding Zen

Recently, groups that practice Zen have thought that Zen is extremely difficult. There are many who hold that it is impossible to do for someone who has a family or who pursues an occupation, and that you can only practice Zen by entering into the mountains and sitting quietly. This view derives from their ignorance of the great dharma, in which all dharmas are nondual.

This is an accurate observation about mistaken views of Zen. Yet people seem unable to abandon the fixed idea that they must find some special place to experience the mystery of Zen. How many are out there at this very moment, wasting so much time and money roaming the world in their search? True, we may able to broaden our knowledge of the Zen and meditation trends of different parts of the world, but not only is it of no help at all in building our own practical Zen powers but we also incur the debts of abandoning our duties and responsibilities in life and even our blessings. What a great loss this is! Such a Zen dharma is of no use to the individual, nor is it any help in developing society or the nation.

At this point, getting on the right road of Zen becomes

very difficult indeed. Instead, we may live out the rest of our days roaming about in search of a method. Or we may finish out our life fruitlessly, without having accomplished anything. The loss, not only to ourselves but to our home, society, and the nation, is equally great.

Furthermore, is it not true that disciplining the mind is disciplining reality, and disciplining reality is disciplining of the mind? So we can experience the effects of disciplining the mind from our disciplining practices within all the different aspects of life: discipline in self-cultivation, discipline of the body, discipline in driving, discipline in sports, discipline in work.

So it is that discipline with favorable sensory conditions, discipline with adverse sensory conditions, discipline in action, and discipline in rest all guarantee the effects of disciplining the mind. If we have rough edges to our personality as we live together with others in our community life, we can achieve harmony with anyone if we discipline our mind, polishing the edges with warmth, filling out the hollows.

What is clear, then, is that each sensory condition provides material for practice and each moment, a chance for practice. One who truly wishes to practice has no reason to shun these precious materials and roam about in search of others.

"All dharmas" here encompasses every relative circumstance.

Right and wrong, good and bad, like and dislike, favorable and adverse, familiar and unfamiliar, action and rest, benefit and harm, self and other, form and void— these and all other relative concepts exist in a relationship of oppositeness, yet their roots are the same. Indeed, from the perspective of Zen practice, they are not separate. About this, the Heart Sutra observes that "form is void and void, form; void is not separate from form, and form is not separate from void." Void exists within form, and form exists together within the void. And so we are told that all dharmas are nondual.

But if one can only practice Zen while sitting but not while standing—this would be a sickly Zen indeed; how could this become the great dharma that can save all sentient beings?

Obviously, we should not lose the Zen mind when we are seated; we must be capable of Zen exertion. At the same time, we must also be able not to lose the Zen mind when standing, going, coming, and working. We can only maintain the Zen mind in all directions when we are capable of Zen exertion in all circumstances; this is the only way for our Zen powers to develop and for us to reap the effects of Zen. This means that perfect Zen powers and efficiency are guaranteed by maintaining the Zen mind equally in both action and rest.

While it may have been said that Zen is best when performed seated, how wasteful it is when we are unable to maintain that mind while also in movement, allowing all manner of disturbance and delusion and wrongdoing to surge forth. This means that one who must be seated, who cannot perform Zen while standing, is like an invalid.

While it may be possible for a seated person to deliver others through Zen, the result is that he or she must forsake the sentient beings who are active in their lives. This, the passage tells us, is "not the answer." When we decide that people in action cannot practice Zen, the touch of deliverance cannot reach them. It is essentially a form of abandonment. It cannot be the great Way.

Zen must be something that the seated person can practice, the standing person can practice, the walking person can practice, the working person can practice— that any person at all can practice—before it can be the great Way that is available to all.

Moreover, since the own-essence of the nature is not merely limited to voidness and calmness alone, if you practice that Zen which is like a senseless thing, this would not be the Zen practice that disciplines the nature but the making of a helpless invalid.

Our fundamental nature is like a seed. By itself, that seed is nothing but a senseless thing, without any life force. It cannot experience the functioning of change. But when the environment around it changes and the conditions become ripe, it displays the wonder of fearsome life. It is not simply an object, capable of nothing. It is a being that contains limitless life force.

That is how self-nature is. Though it is rooted in voidness and calmness, it contains all possibilities. They remain contained until the conditions are ripe, and then they display fearsome power. They mature as we discipline them, and develop as we guide them. It is not a being that is rigidly restricted to voidness and calmness. It is one that contains all the elements for limitless possibility.

"Practicing that Zen which is like a senseless thing" refers to the kind of Zen that buries all of these possibilities. This type of Zen is described as being like a senseless thing because we leave behind the perspective of disciplining the nature and become fixated only on the Zen dharma, or the attempt to do nothing at all.

In the first instance, and also the second, Zen is about disciplining our nature. As need dictates, we must discipline ourselves with not doing and with doing. Discipline also comes in thousands and myriads of different forms; the content of our discipline will differ in as many forms as there are circumstances. Yet although this is the situation, we cannot even fathom all discipline if we believe the answer lies in not doing this or that. What a powerless thing we become! So this passage warns us: To fixate on the Zen that is like a senseless thing is not Zen practice but something that makes us into helpless invalids.

Therefore, even when involved in disturbing situations, the mind should be undisturbed; even when involved with greed-creating sensory conditions, the mind should be unmoving—this is true Zen and true purity.

Someone who is skilled at swimming does not drown when he or she is underwater. Someone even more skilled enjoys the waves when he or she is in their midst. One who is skilled at driving can drive freely and autonomously, even when traffic conditions are difficult.

Gold may be befouled with waste, yet its nature never changes; it remains untainted. Its essence does not become soiled; all we have to do is wash it off with water. The great rock valley remains unshaken by the fierce water.

This is what Zen power is like. However noisy its surroundings may be, it never becomes as noisy or disturbed. However buried we may be in sensory conditions of wealth, sex, fame, or gain, our mind does not move, nor is it tainted. This is spiritual power. No sensory condition can do anything against the mind that is centered like an iron pillar. The sensory conditions are as the sensory conditions are, and the mind is as the mind is. Indeed, those sensory conditions are simply a training ground, a testing site for disciplining the mind. The roiling waves of sensory conditions are but a playground for experiencing the joys of Zen.

This realm is the realm of the one who is not roiled by sounds and forms nor shaken by the favorable and adverse. This is the approach of the true practitioner: There is no enticement or obstruction in any affair, and we unfold endlessly the creative transformations of marvelous existence as we freely engage in prosperous activities.

VII. The Main Principles of Zen

To reiterate the main principles of timeless Sŏn:
"When the six sense organs are free from activity,
remove distracting thoughts and nurture the one mind.
When the six sense organs are involved in activity,
remove the wrong and nurture the right."

So far, I have been trying to provide a general
understanding of Zen through the text of the "Dharma of
Timeless Zen," illuminating the purport of Timeless Zen,
the main principles of the Zen dharma, the practical issues
of Zen and their results, and prejudices that may exist.

The last, main principles of methodology that the text
gives for entering real Zen consist of the dharma of Zen
when we are free from activity and the dharma of Zen
when we are involved in activity.

As we live in this world, all things that come from the
functioning of our six sense organs may be boiled down
to the times when we are involved in activity and those
when we are free from activity. There are only these two:
times when we are involved in activity, and times when
we are free from activity. What determines the course of
this life, and our eternal lives, is whether we act in accor-

dance with regulations in these two instances.

The dharma of Timeless Zen is intended to show us how to make the best use of these two situations. It is also a method for achieving limitless growth for ourselves within these two situations. It also exists to help us maximize the efficiency of the things in which we are involved so that we succeed in all things, and to help us maximize the resulting merits.

With these two types of situation, then, we must evaluate each situation appropriately and proceed in the following manner: removing distracting thoughts and nurturing an integrated mind when we are free from activity, and removing the wrong and nurturing the right when we are involved in activity.

At times, it is quite unclear just what kind of boundary exists between times when we are involved in activity and times when we are free from activity. This is what is meant by the six sense organs being "involved" or "free." The only time when the six sense organs are truly resting is when we sleep. Other than that, at least some part of our six sense organs is functioning. There is no moment when the functioning of the six sense organs has completely ceased.

This is why we must be capable of recognizing and understanding exactly what is meant by "involved in activity" and "free from activity." We could easily misunderstand it, and take it to mean "when we are asleep" and "when we are awake." Moreover, we must also have a proper understanding of the concepts of "distracting thoughts," "one mind," "wrong," and "right" before we begin our practice. Otherwise, we might enter with a mistaken understanding and suffer the consequences.

When we misunderstand the concepts of "distracting thoughts" and "one mind," "wrong" and "right," or "involved in activity" and "free from activity," we may wander aimlessly and fail to reach the truth of Zen; we may hesitate, or never move beyond the idea of postponing it as "something to do next time." We must also be very wary of remaining stuck in thoughts that are complicated or vague.

But when we achieve a sufficient understanding of the concepts, and when we proceed after having profoundly examined the methods of Zen, the methods themselves are not at all difficult. Indeed, they are something that any of us can do easily in our daily life. We must, however, have the functioning of belief, zeal, questioning, and dedication.

Great Principles of Zen

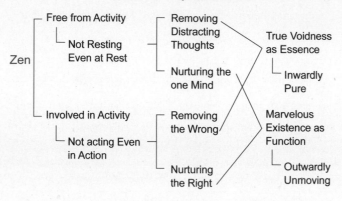

Indeed, these qualities of belief, zeal, questioning, and dedication should be functioning not only in Zen but in anything meaningful in which we are involved. In other words, we should proceed with a clear conviction about the meaning or outcome of what we are doing, and then resolve ourselves to do it and exert ourselves. We should then arouse the questioning mind to search for a method to do it well, and proceed with steady commitment once we have received a definite answer. If we do this, we will succeed in all that we do.

The same is true for Zen. A conviction about the need for Zen must be established first before the exertion to practice Zen, one way of another, will come into action. If we begin our Zen practice with this exertion, we will inevitably come to ask questions, such as "What we are supposed to do?"

and we cannot fail to resolve these questions. Once we have obtained an answer to our questions, we must then begin our Zen practice and show steady commitment to it before we reap the effects of Zen practice. Thus, the qualities of belief, zeal, questioning, and dedication are necessary conditions for the process of Zen practice.

Before we move on, I would like to summarize these six concepts: freedom from activity and involvement in activity, the one mind and distracting thoughts, and right and wrong.

Here, I am simply stating the most important parts of the meanings of these six concepts and connecting them once again to the main principles of the dharma of Timeless Zen with a diagram. My hope is that this will help the Zen practitioner to avoid wandering and proceed directly to grasping the gist of the dharma of Timeless Zen.

Once we have sufficiently understood these concepts, we must then begin our Zen practice according to the concepts that we have illuminated. In other words, we must respond to each and every affair from the standpoint of utterly removing the wrong and nurturing the right when we are involved in activity.

When we are free from activity, we must proceed by responding from moment to moment from the standpoint of utterly removing distracting thoughts and nurturing the one mind.

What the Concepts Mean

INVOLVEMENT IN ACTIVITY
When we are doing something with someone else When we are carrying out our duties When we are performing work and activities When we are confronted with external conditions
THE ONE MIND
The mind that evaluating appropriately The focused mind The mind that remains level The mind that is reined in The mind that is aware of its subjectivity The mind that is consistent The mind that is unbent The mind that puts things in order
RIGHT
That which is grace to the self and others That which is rational That which is based in fact That which serves as a standard to commend That which requites grace That which obeys the law That which upholds the precepts That which is timely That which conforms to etiquette That which is impartial in its behavior That which is natural for the characteristics of each individual affair

FREEDOM FROM ACTIVITY

When we are spending time on our own
When we have stopped working on our duties
When we have finished our work and activities
When we are together with internal conditions

DISTRACTING THOUGHTS

The mind that lacks a standard of evaluation
The mind that is scattered in all directions
The mind that wanders without a direction
The mind that is not reined in
The mind that has only a blurry notion of its subjectivity
The intermittent mind
The wicked mind
The negligent mind

WRONG

That which causes harm to the self and others
That which is irrational
That which contradicts fact
That which serves as a norm for prohibition
That which commits ingratitude
That which defies the law
That which breaks the precepts
That which does not conform to the time and restraints
That which violates etiquette
That which is clinging and fixated
That which is not right for the characteristics of
each individual affair

Free from Activity: Removing Distracting Thoughts and Nurturing the One Mind

As a general concept, "distracting thoughts" refers to random thoughts, untimely thoughts, thoughts suffused with the three poisons and five desires, and thoughts that are obscured by appearances.

In the context of seated meditation, all thoughts are distracting thoughts when they are not holding the mind in the elixir field. The right mind is the mind that rests where we wish our mind to rest, and all other minds are distracted by thoughts. Even when our thoughts are right, they are, at that moment, distracting thoughts.

These distracting thoughts cause great torment to our mind when we wish to practice Zen. No sooner do we think that we have driven them away than they return. They come again, and it seems uncertain whether there will ever come a time when we can put all these distracting thoughts to rest.

It may seem to us that it is all but impossible to remove distracting thoughts completely. The effort seems to be an endless repetition of victory followed by defeat.

The dharma of Timeless Zen tells us of the mind that we must establish in ourselves until this time comes. It advises us not to let go of the spirit that fights to the bitter end.

Free from Activity

When we are spending time on our own
When we have stopped working on our duties
When we have finished our work and other activities
When we are together with internal conditions

Nurturing the One Mind

The mind that evaluates appropriately

The focused mind

The mind that remains level

The mind that is reined in

The mind that is aware of its subjectivity

The mind that is consistent

The unbent mind

The mind that puts things in order

Distracting Thoughts

The mind that does not evaluate appropriately

The mind that is scattered in all directions

The mind that wanders without direction

The unbridled mind

The mind that has only a blurry notion of its subjectivity

The intermittent mind

The wicked mind

The negligent mind

A fight with our physical body leaves wounds; a fight with our mind leaves a scar of deep despondency. In the case of a wound on our body, we take steps to prevent germs from invading, and it heals over time. The same is true for wounds to the mind. As long as we avoid the danger of succumbing to the powerlessness of resignation, time will resolve the problem.

So it is that the practitioner must not only encourage the spirit of fighting to the end, but also establish the one mind that evaluates the situation appropriately as we respond, taking every distracting thought that comes and thinking, "A moment for practice has arrived."

Before we can remove distracting thoughts, though, we must first notice that the distracting thoughts have entered. The arrival of a distracting thought is evidence that we have let go of the mind that evaluates appropriately; once we have reestablished appropriate evaluation, the distracting thought will go away by itself. It is like a darkened room: No amount of sweeping will drive the darkness away. The darkness disappears on its own. So it is with the mind: Once we evaluate them appropriately, the distracting thoughts go away by themselves.

If we follow what is given in the above diagram for "Free from Activity," then we must act, act, and act yet more, working endlessly to accumulate merits.

I would also like to add an explanation here on the mistaken tendency to seek the nurturing of the one mind through reciting the Buddha's name and performing seated meditation alone.

There is no one single method for nurturing the one mind. There are several. Many dharmas of cultivation exist that are capable of nurturing the one mind in any circumstance. Indeed, those dharmas are the dharma of Mahāyāna meditation; they are a Zen dharma that promotes efficiency, so that we can engage in both work and practice together and reap the effects.

This means that we should find the things that present strong potential for guiding us to the one mind and then practice the one mind while doing those things. We should find things in which we have an interest, the things that are necessary, the things that we happen to want to do, and focus the one mind on each of them. This can be very effective. We find things that are light, things that do not make intensive demands of choice between right and wrong, and we focus our one mind there. For instance, we may pursue samādhi through reading, calligraphy, music, or work.

Someone who is less versed in practice may, in moments of leisure, spend all of his or her time fruitlessly amid all manner of perverse states of mind and distracting thoughts. This is why we are advised to be wary when we are on our own. A person with a skill for practice makes effective use of moments of leisure.

When we are busy, we discipline ourselves well with the things that preoccupy us. By doing this, we amass great powers. Let us look at three situations that are absolutely necessary if we are to reap the effects of removing distracting thoughts and nurturing the one mind.

The first of them is to recite the Buddha's name, chant incantations, and perform seated meditation (the subjective one mind).

Recitation of the Buddha's name, incantations, and seated meditation are all specialized elements of this practice. As we immerse ourselves in the one mind of recitation, the one mind of incantation, and the one mind of meditation, all distracting thoughts are removed and the subjective one mind is nurtured. This is the Zen dharma by which we become fully aware of our subjective inner world, pushing forward with the one mind.*

Second is formal prayer (the one mind of pledging).

Formal prayer is a ritual of offering up a great pledge. It offers us a shortcut to guiding our mind to the one

---

* Please refer here to the commentary on methods of seated meditation in the *Principal Book*.

mind. The greater and more heartfelt our pledge, the better the one mind will be. If we cannot achieve the one mind, the formal prayer itself will not work. Because the pledge itself is the epicenter for producing the one mind, the one mind is not achieved very easily, but it is accompanied by an effect of clustering aspirational power. Because aspirational power is the motive force for all action, it is the key element that the practitioner must first establish.

The third situation is when we are working (the one mind in work).

When we are working, our priority must be on removing the wrong and nurturing the right, but we should also pursue the effects of removing distracting thoughts and nurturing the one mind. In other words, we remove distracting thoughts when we are not drawn to something else when we are working on something, and we nurture the one mind when we focus on that thing alone. If we accumulate merits by focusing on each individual thing, whatever that thing happens to be, then our work will succeed, and we will build the strength to easily achieve the one mind in any situation.

We should examine here the dharma instruction on the four approaches to the mind, which is something we must refer to as we build the one mind. These approaches are the following: seizing the mind, watching the mind, no mind, and the able mind.

Seizing the mind is the approach whereby we bind the mind to some place. Like tying the willful calf to a stake, it is the state of taking steps to ensure that the mind remains in one place, that it does not run freely and without any restrictions. We are speaking here of reciting the Buddha's name, performing seated meditation, or offering formal prayer, or any other practice to discipline our concentration and keep it tied to one place.

Watching the mind is like a parent watching after a small child. The practitioner is looking at his or her own mind. When parents view their child, it is with a mind full of love. They protect the child from dangerous places and help the child play well. Even when the child makes mistakes, they do not criticize. They simply protect and prevent with their love, helping the child grow up well. They feed, they clothe, they tuck in, they play together, they bathe, they wipe, and they look after the child in all sorts of ways. The wise parent does not criticize a child for crying; the parent simply looks for the cause of the crying and responds to it.

Thus, wise parents are unswerving in their attention to the child. Similarly, wise practitioners know to keep a good eye on the mind. They watch it with a mind that is unconditionally loving even when the mind is still in an untamed state. And so they protect it from dangerous places and keep it in acceptable places; they tend to its needs. They show particular concern. And as we follow the procedure and take rigorous measures with our mind, it becomes gradually tamed. This is watching the mind.

No mind is the practice of emptying the mind completely. We are ridding it of all distracting and silly thoughts, of all disturbance and delusion and wrongdoing, of all the thoughts that produce greed, anger, or delusion. We do and let go; we have and let go; we let go and yet let go of letting go, until we fully achieve unity with the true nature of nothingness, and then we let go of the notion of having unified.

The **able mind** has let go and let go until there is nothing left to let go of, yet it must also be capable of seizing as the need arises. This is called "autonomy of seizing and releasing." We have achieved great liberation, without being bound to any one thing, yet we must also have the power of freedom and autonomy before we have fully restored our sovereignty. It is the practitioner's ideal: the state of sovereignty for the future having been restored, the attainment of the wish-fulfilling gem.

As we continue accumulating these merits, our Zen practice will gradually mature, and we will achieve single-practice samādhi and *Il-Sang* samādhi with one suchness in action and rest, so that we are able to roam amid the adverse and favorable, action and rest, in the realm of all samādhis.

Involved in Activity: Removing the Wrong and Nurturing the Right

Human life is a veritable whirlpool of right and wrong, benefit and harm. As we live in its midst, gradually building the power of the right and gradually weakening the power of the wrong are not only essential from a character standpoint but also highly important essentials for society.

Yet in reality we cannot do it. We have two types of mind: the human mind and the mind of the Way. The human mind is the instinctual mind, which emerges from its basis in our body, and the mind of the Way is the mind of our original nature, which emerges from its basis in the self-nature. For this reason, a person cannot help but have the mind that is based in the physical body, and cannot help but have the mind that is based in our fundamental nature.

In other words, we have both the instincts of the physical body and the original nature of our fundamental essence existing together. When the instincts of the physical body reign supreme, the original nature cannot exercise its strength; when the original nature seizes powerful initiative, the instincts of the physical body cannot run riot.

It is here where right and wrong lie rooted, until sensory conditions arrive and they manifest whichever way the greater power lies. This means that when wrong is powerful—the characteristic of the perverse mind—it operates and gains supremacy when we encounter places (sensory conditions) in which that powerful force is used. Conversely, when right is strong—the characteristic of the mind of the Way—it operates when we encounter places in which that powerful force is used. It overcomes the wrong and seizes supremacy.

At these times, if a practitioner mobilizes his or her belief, zeal, questioning, and dedication to boldly repel the wrong, as identified in the following diagram, and establishes the mind of surely building the power of right, then this is what is meant by nurturing the right.

We must work so that the right gains strength, be it in the individual or in society. This is not a matter of practicing what is right at any one moment; the power of right is nurtured as we repeat solely the practice of what is right in matters both large and small.

Involved in Activity

When we are doing something with someone else
When we are executing our duties
When we are performing work and activities
When we are confronted with external conditions

Nurturing the Right

That which is grace to the self and others
That which is rational
That which is based in fact
That which serves as a standard to commend
That which requites grace
That which obeys the law
That which upholds the precepts
That which is timely
That which conforms to etiquette
That which is impartial in its behavior
That which is natural for the characteristics of each individual affair

Removing the Wrong

That which causes harm to the self and others
That which is irrational
That which contradicts fact
That which serves as a norm for prohibition
That which is ungrateful
That which defies the law
That which breaks the precepts
That which does not conform to time and restraints
That which violates etiquette
That which is clinging and fixated
That which is not right for the characteristics of each individual affair

Finally, we will be able to achieve the awesome power of implementation. Every kind of power is nurtured as we repeat it.

Thus the power of right, too, is nurtured in repeated practice of what is right. Nurturing what is right is a matter of repeating only right action, without discriminating between big and small.

With society and with the individual, the power of what is right is strengthened as we mature with our skill at managing right and wrong. Conversely, if our skill at managing right and wrong fails to mature, then the power of wrong will grow relatively stronger, and we will all find ourselves in the unfortunate situation of having no recourse when we are swept along by the wrong.

At these moments, we must exercise powerful belief, zeal, questioning, and dedication, repeating the practice of what is right and fighting to the end in matters both big and small.

In the fight of right and wrong, we cannot allow ourselves what we do or how we feel to be dictated by success or failure. We should not become arrogant over our victories; still less should we abandon ourselves over our defeats. We must fight to the end without being arrogant or abandoning ourselves.

In the process, the power of wrong will gradually

diminish, until finally and surely the wrong is removed, and the right sounds the victory drum and takes its assured place.

For this reason, we should work to accumulate merits with ceaselessly repeated discipline according to the above diagram for when we are free from activity or involved in activity.

For every part of the practice of eliminating the wrong and nurturing the right according to the spirit explained above, there are areas that demand caution.

First, we must examine the process of setting our plan. In everything we do, we should examine it from the planning stages to determine if its purpose is right or wrong. If it is righteous, we should gladly choose and pursue it, but if it is wrong or impure motives lurk in any part of it at all, we must have the resolution to boldly abandon it or let it go.

We should also refer to this when we are choosing our future or selecting a profession. If its direction is one of grace to ourselves and others, then we should follow it without hesitation, but if it is a profession or future that does harm to anyone or is predicated on sacrifice, then it is better for us to abandon that choice.

There are also things here that confuse us. They are traps of temptation: Even when something is not right, they tell us that by doing them, we can produce a golden egg, get a windfall, or find good fortune. Someone who is foolish and greedy will be unable to escape those traps. He or she will be fully taken in by lures that come packaged with specious pretexts. In the end, he or she will merely be deceived. In some cases, he or she will succumb to awful failure or sin in the mire of transgression.

Beginnings are crucial. It is said that starting is half the battle—in other words, by beginning with a wise decision, we have already achieved half of our success. So if we begin by deciding on a plan that is based in righteousness, whatever we do afterward to pursue it will be righteous as well. We must therefore be very careful with our beginnings.

The word "righteous" here is often used in conjunction with "rightfulness" and "rationality." If something is truly rightful, then it will also be rational, and if something is truly rational, then it will also be rightful. This is rightness and wisdom.

Second, we should examine the process of our work to see if it is right or wrong. In the West, there is a saying about "stealing a candle to read the Bible." It is a kind mind, obviously, that wishes to read the Bible, but this does not justify stealing a candle. It cannot be argued that any process at all is just because its aims are right.

Moreover, temptations to use various "secret methods" may lurk in the process of doing what is right. Those temptations always lay out bait in the form of personal gain or interests. To brush aside those temptations and choose the right is not something that just anyone can do. The practitioner, however, must be able to boldly spurn them. At such times, we truly need the power of the right. The person with the practitioner's capabilities of conduct will not commit a wrong even if doing so will give him or her the whole world. This is a truly righteous person. With all the destruction of others for our own interests in the world today, with all the crowds who will use the failures of others as an opportunity to advance themselves, we are truly in need of practice to remove the wrong and nurture the right.

As difficult as the reality may be, and whatever transformations the situation may undergo, we must always respond to the reality from the standpoint of removing the wrong and nurturing the right.

Third, we should examine our work once it is completed. After we have finished our work, we should look over the entire process from the beginning to see if any mistakes were made in terms of removing the wrong and nurturing the right. We should also look to see if we have cleanly attended to any follow-up measures needed for the products of our work. Once the work is complete, we have to examine whether the results were righteous. Indeed, our assessment of the process may change according to the outcome that resulted from it.

Moreover, the result is not fully complete with the outcome. Instead, it functions as a new beginning, as the seed of future results. Our handling of the products must be truly righteous if we are to avoid regrets.

We human beings feel tension in our beginnings and in our processes. Even when we comport ourselves with caution, we release all our tension when a result emerges. In this case, we become arrogant when we succeed, and we try to keep things to ourselves, or we lose our self-control. When we fail, we feel frustrated and preoccupy ourselves with trying to shed all responsibility. All of this is a matter of succumbing to foolishness, of clipping the buds of hope at a new beginning.

This stems from a lack of practice with removing the wrong and nurturing the right. It is our misfortune. We must be very wary of the fact that unwholesome causes may spring from good results, and wholesome causes from bad results. Indeed, the person who understands surely that each good result harbors poisons, and that each bad result harbors a ray of hope is a wise person who can effectively distinguish between right and wrong.

Not only must we do a good job of examining our results, but we must also examine our handling of the results and eliminate any deviation from the principle of removing the wrong and nurturing the right that exists anywhere in it.

In the beginning, then, removing the wrong and nurturing the right originate from actions. They apply to every last word, and later to every last thought and mind. Each action, each word, and each thought must be scrutinized again and again according to the principle of removing the wrong and nurturing the right. The wrong must be cleaned like the void, and the right must be firmly established like Mount T'ai.

This is all that I am going to say in terms of commenting on the general principles of the main text of the dharma of Timeless Zen. But because the terms *timeless* and *placeless* encompass such a broad range of times and every type of situation that unfolds within space, it is not a matter that can be fully explained with the commentary thus far.

To ensure that our practice of the dharma of Timeless Zen is accurate and efficient, we were given the "Practice" chapter of the *Principal Book* and the dharma instruction on practice in the *Scripture of the Founding Master*. I would like to use that content to present the relationships of the principles in diagram format, with a little explanation of my own. Because the practice of the dharma of Timeless Zen does not involve distinctions of time or place, it must be approached from a variety of angles, as it is a Zen practice that encompasses all domains in all directions: all circumstances of limitless action in limitless space and limitless time.

In the "Practice" chapter of the *Principal Book* and the "Practice" chapter of the *Scripture of the Founding Master*, we find the answer.

CHAPTER TWO

THE DHARMA OF TIMELESS ZEN AND THE NINE ARTICLES OF THE ESSENTIAL DHARMAS OF DAILY PRACTICE

The great principle of the *Won*-Buddhist doctrine centers on the truth of the O, the Fourfold Grace (Heaven and Earth, Parents, Fellow Beings, and Laws), the Four Essentials (developing self-power, the primacy of the wise, educating others' children, and venerating the public-spirited), the Threefold Study (cultivating the spirit, inquiry into human affairs and universal principles, and choice in action), and the Eight Articles (developing belief, zeal, questioning, and dedication, and forsaking unbelief, greed, laziness, and foolishness). All of these principles of the order's rites are laid out for us to discipline ourselves in our daily life. In this way, we have been allowed to reap the effects of Timeless Zen—removing distracting thoughts and nurturing the one mind, removing the wrong and nurturing the right—as we compare and test ourselves against the nine articles of the Essential Dharmas of Daily Practice and repeat our practice of them.

It is in that sense that I have presented the dharma of Timeless Zen and the Nine Articles in diagram format. The Essential Dharmas of Daily Practice truly represent

Dharma of Timeless Zen

Free from Activity
Involved in Activity

Removing Distracting Thoughts

Nurturing the One Mind

Giving rise to purity of the self-nature

So that we remain free from disturbance by sensory conditions

Giving rise to the wisdom of the self-nature

So that we remain free from being deluded by sensory conditions

Giving rise to the precepts of the self-nature

So that we remain free from wrongdoing as we encounter sensory conditions

Removing unbelief, greed, laziness, and foolishness

With belief, zeal, questioning, and dedication

Removing the Wrong

Nurturing the Right

Settling accounts with our life of resentment

Practicing the life of gratitude

Settling accounts with the life of other-power

With a life of self-power

Settling accounts with the life of no learning

With the life of learning

Settling accounts with the life of no teaching

With the life of teaching

Settling accounts with the life of no concern for public welfare

With the life of concern for public welfare

The Dharma of Timeless Zen and the Nine Articles of the Essential Dharmas of Daily Practice a marvelous method for disciplining ourselves with the myriad of wisdoms, myriad of abilities, and myriad of virtues of the tathāgata. The words may seem simple, and the articles may number only nine, but they are concepts that encompass the full breadth of the doctrine. They present all of the necessary conditions for the tathāgata. Those who are capable of following them will, even in their dealings with the stubbornness of sentient beings, be tathāgatas with myriad of powers of deliverance.

Though the list includes just nine ordinary articles, they are accompanied by many sublime meanings and encompass the basic elements that allow limitless growth. Moreover, they also represent a marvelous method that can be applied to managing a healthy organization or group of any kind.

It is clear, in other words, that they are essential conditions for any sort of circumstance in an individual's practice, or in the development of an organization or group. If we establish a deep interest in them, it is clear that they will bring not only great blessings for ourselves but auspicious imports for every place in which their meaning dwells.

As we faithfully practice the Essential Dharmas of Daily Practice, then, the elements of the dharma of Timeless Zen—removing distracting thoughts and nurturing the one mind, removing the wrong and nurturing the right—will happen of their own accord. This truly is the essence of the dharma of Timeless Zen.

The text thus tells us that we need only recite and recite again the Essential Dharmas of Daily Practice, practice them, and practice them more, and this will suffice for us to achieve buddhahood.

We all, as human beings and not just practitioners, should allow these Nine Articles of the Essential Dharmas of Daily Practice to become a part of us, to establish themselves in our character. This is all the more crucial when we are someone with the aim of achieving great things. They must truly serve as a standard for living throughout all lives.

Among them, the first, second, and third articles are the core, the items that the practitioner should regard as essential items for daily living, something that we keep closest to us as we live our life. Here I feel that something of a basic explanation is warranted.

With the first, second, and third articles, we must begin with a basic understanding in four stages as we start our practice.

Stage 1: Understanding the mind-ground

Stage 2: Understanding sensory conditions

Stage 3: Understanding freedom from disturbance, delusion, and wrongdoing

Stage 4: Understanding giving rise to purity, wisdom, and precepts of the self-nature

Stage 1: Understanding the Mind-Ground

The mind-ground is the foundation on which the mind is based, before a single thought has emerged. Before any thoughts emerge, there is nothing there. Sometimes this realm is referred to as "the spirit" or "nature," but its true form is a world where no perfect expression, no matter how we word it, is possible.

This is why the mind-ground is referred to as being "beyond all words and speech." For at the original foundation of the mind, there is no disturbance, no delusion, no wrongdoing, nor anything else at all; it is like the original ground with nothing upon it. When it meets the right mixture of moisture and temperature, various weeds begin to sprout. Before anything, we must have a definite understanding of the characteristics of the mind-ground, how the original mind is free from anything, but how various thoughts arise when it encounters sensory conditions. We must also have a detailed understanding of how it connects with karma, and of all the limitless linkages with cause and effect.

Stage 2: Understanding Sensory Conditions

Sensory conditions are the sum total of the real-world situations that unfold outside, irrespective of ourselves. They merely perform their individual functions as their characteristics dictate; it is in the process of their entering inside us, the formation of karmic consciousness through receiving, thinking, and acting, that the various conscious minds of discrimination arise. In form, all of these disturbances, delusions, and instances of wrongdoing arise like blades of grass. Depending on our minds, then, sensory conditions may be typhoons, or they may be mild breezes. They may be tigers, and they may be tiny insects. They may be treasures of grace, or they may be mere tatters of tissue paper. They may produce limitless value, or they may produce limitless damage. View them positively and they are like the scent of flowers; view them negatively and they are but weeds. All of these are questions of the subjective mind that receives them. In this way, we cycle through an endless process of disturbance, delusion, and wrongdoing, arising and disappearing like blades of grass as we encounter sensory conditions.

Stage 3: Freedom from Disturbance, Delusion, and Wrongdoing

As we watch these minds arising like blades of grass with sensory conditions, we must strive to quickly notice the first sign of being drawn or tilting toward disturbance, delusion, or wrongdoing and eliminate it. We are like the farmer who rushes to pluck the weeds sprouting up in his rice paddy. If, like that diligent farmer, we give the weeds no space to grow, the grain will eventually grow so profusely that there is nowhere left for the weeds to sprout.

In this way, one who practices well works busily to remove any distracting thoughts that arise—disturbance, delusion, and wrongdoing, as well as belief, greed, laziness, and foolishness—and gives them no place to set root. In the process, wisdom will gradually grow to fill the field of the mind, so that we produce only immeasurable blessings.

There is something of which we must be wary at this moment. It is the mind that is deeply anguished by the distracting thoughts that seem to arise at every moment. The more we anguish, the more the perverse states of minds and distracting thoughts will rage. The mind, watching all of this unfold, will ultimately succumb to resignation.

No matter how many perverse states of mind and distracting thoughts may arise, we must face them with a readiness to dismiss them as mere weeds in fertile growth and seize them at the earliest opportunity. Taking care of them at the earliest sign is the easiest method of dealing with them.

To do this, there is a certain ability that we need. Just as weeds will have no ground to grow on if we tend our rice plants and help them grow profusely, so these thoughts will have nowhere to set root if when we are filled with dedication, the mind of faith, the public spirit, the mind of practice, the mind of compassion and loving-kindness. This is a great skill, but practice is not merely a matter of imitation. It is essential that we mobilize practical efforts based solely on the truth: belief, zeal, questioning, and dedication. We must be very wary.

Stage 4: Understanding Giving Rise to Purity, Wisdom, and Precepts of the Self-Nature

In every one of us, the self-nature already possesses purity, wisdom, and precepts. When we do not harness the power of these things—even though they are there— we are like a small child who has ears, eyes, a nose, a mouth, and four limbs yet is incapable of independence. As in raising a small child, we must take various measures so that the original attributes of the self-nature gain strength. As we enrich it substantively with processes in our daily routine, and with fixed-term and daily training, the child develops strength before we know it. If we lapse into formalism, only the shell will take shape; we must approach it practically in both the first instance and the second. "Giving rise" here refers to bringing our purity, wisdom, and precepts to a level of such firm entrenchment and solidity that they cannot collapse, no matter what the circumstances are.

There are three essential attributes that the true self-nature possesses: purity, wisdom, and precepts. These three essential attributes are something that we certainly possess, but their practical powers are still weak. When we encounter sensory conditions, our purity is shaken, our wisdom is obscured, and our precepts collapse, sending our character hurtling toward catastrophe.

Before this tragic situation comes about, we should make it our practice to build our powers of purity, wisdom, and precepts so that we finally establish a substance and attributes of the self-nature that are firm and unyielding, centered like an iron pillar and defended like a stone wall.

The practice by which we can achieve this is the practice dharma of progressing in concert with the Threefold Study, and the practice dharmas of Timeless Zen and Placeless Zen.

CHAPTER THREE

THE DHARMA OF TIMELESS ZEN
AND FIXED-TERM TRAINING

Cultivating the dharma of Timeless Zen in our daily life may be the greater principle, but our minds have an aspect that we truly cannot understand. As we live buried in sensory conditions, without realizing it, we become obscured, attached, and tainted. Deep fissures arise, and though we are sinking deep into some place, we do not realize that it is happening. We slide deeper still because we are unaware. The further we sink, the more impossibly difficult it becomes to extricate ourselves. We succumb to riches and honors, we succumb to shackles of poverty and disadvantage, we succumb to proximity and distance, to favor and disfavor. We succumb to pleasure, anger, sorrow, and joy, or to worry and anguish. The deeper we fall, the harder the clusters of karma form, and the more they become like shackles that bind us. At this point, we become slaves to the karmic clusters, without hope of escape, not hesitating to let the wheels of the cycle of six destinies catch us and drag us onto unwholesome paths. We have truly fallen into a slough of despondency.

The dharma of fixed-term training is what the

Founding Master provided for us as a breakthrough, a way of rescuing us from this danger. Whatever we may do in our daily life, we are, for the period of fixed-term training, to drop all things and receive expert training.

On the days of the regular dharma meeting, we are to set aside all of our everyday practices and attend, attend, attend, without exception. This in itself is discipline for liberation. As we make sure to appear for every dharma meeting, and as we practice—once, twice, for a year, for two years, for ten years, for a lifetime—we gain the strength of releasing and doing. The power of liberation and freedom that comes from freely and autonomously releasing and doing all things is truly awesome.

Moreover, when we set aside a period during the year for special, fixed-term training, and then set aside all things (our daily life) to participate in fixed-term training, completing every one of the designated fixed-term training courses, we gain limitlessly from the new feeling that emerges, from the realization, the taming, and the practical abilities. By merely resolving to put aside everything and take part in fixed-term Zen, we are seizing the initiative for our own liberation.

The fixed-term Zen in which we participate is a form of practice that requires three things together: our vow, preparation, and resolution. Because we must enter it as a blank slate, having set down all honors, status, authority, pride, and even knowledge, the entire process is itself material for practice and discipline. The reward that we reap, without even realizing it, is accordingly rich. Some people of high status or who have many children may find it difficult to take part in fixed-term Zen. This is evidence of how they are in thrall to knowledge and status. When you are in thrall, liberation is impossible.

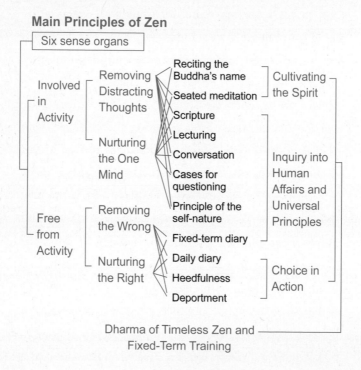

Main Principles of Zen

Six sense organs

Involved in Activity

Removing Distracting Thoughts

Nurturing the One Mind

Reciting the Buddha's name

Seated meditation

Scripture

Lecturing

Conversation

Cases for questioning

Cultivating the Spirit

Inquiry into Human Affairs and Universal Principles

Free from Activity

Removing the Wrong

Nurturing the Right

Principle of the self-nature

Fixed-term diary

Daily diary

Heedfulness

Deportment

Choice in Action

Dharma of Timeless Zen and Fixed-Term Training

This means that fixed-term Zen and fixed-term training are themselves the dharma of Timeless Zen.

Moreover, by establishing a year, ten years, a lifetime of giving our fullest dedication to each one of these subjects, we will have truly assured ourselves of the status of buddha and bodhisattva.

I will omit an explanation here of each one of the items in fixed-term training; details are presented in the "Training Dharma" section of the *Principal Book*. I also truly recommend that you participate in the training offered by training organizations. You should make sure to participate not just once but as a yearly event.

If you do so, you will receive limitless dharma grace. Your participation itself is practice for release and liberation. Accordingly, you can reap the effects of new realization and no longer being obscured.

There is also the dharma of the diary, which follows from fixed-term and daily training. Unfortunately, I cannot give a detailed introduction, but you will receive ample introduction to it during the fixed-term training period, so I am omitting that here.

I will only say that this diary dharma contains information about preventing outflows during the practice progress, and about encouraging exertion in practice, examination of the process, and guiding realization. For details about the methods, I encourage you to refer to it yourselves.

What, then, of pursuing mind practice at a Zen center?

1. It is a way in which we can tie the cavorting calf to a stake, tame it as it grows, and gradually come to use that calf in the future in accordance with our own will.

2. It is a way in which the sufferer of the mind disease can enter the mind hospital for treatment, creating a self that is replete with health while also becoming the Medicine King who will treat the great diseases under heaven in the future.

3. By entering "military school" and studying and discipling ourselves with ways of pacifying the mind's chaos, we polish the vision of the commander who will pacify the great chaos of the world in the future.

4. By cultivating and developing the fallow mind field, we create fields of blessings, which we can cultivate to produce great harvests in the future.

5. By shedding the failings of the sentient being and becoming buddhas and bodhisattvas, we are assured a future of infinite kalpas and can practice visions without limit for delivering sentient beings and curing the world.

This practice is thus the most fundamental practice and the greatest practice, a practice that we cannot fail to perform once our perception has awakened.

CHAPTER FOUR

THE DHARMA OF TIMELESS ZEN AND THE ITEMS OF HEEDFULNESS IN DAILY APPLICATIONS

The word *timeless* is much the same thing as *daily*. The timeless is daily and the daily, timeless. The Items of Heedfulness in Daily Applications are six conditions for achieving the dharma of Timeless Zen without fail. If the main principles of the dharma of Timeless Zen are removing distracting thoughts, nurturing the one mind, removing the wrong, and nurturing the right, then to achieve this we must do the following.

First, choose with whole and sound thought.

Often, a person who encounters sensory conditions will respond spontaneously and reflexively. We make rash choices, ill-considered choices, choices that are swayed by karmic power, and we either commit grave errors or we roll a new wheel in the cycle of six destinies.

After we have restored wholeness and soundness by simply stopping after encountering any kind of sensory condition, thinking with a whole and sound mind to make a right determination and thus achieving an accurate and correct determination, we utterly remove what we suspect is wrong, and we choose and put into practice what we believe is right. In so doing, we are removing idle thoughts and nurturing only the one mind. Choosing with whole and sound thought is thus one of the essential preconditions of the dharma of Timeless Zen.

If we neglect this precondition, hardly anything will turn out right. To achieve this, we are instructed to focus on the practice of mindfulness. Mindfulness practice means choosing with whole and sound thought in each and every thing that we have to do. When we do this, it is mindfulness; if we do not, it is unmindfulness. There are, however, two stages of standards that we apply in examining our mindfulness or unmindfulness.

The first stage is examining presence or absence with a heedful mind. We are still withholding an examination of whether our affairs were well done or mistaken; instead, we are simply examining with a heedful mind to look for presence or absence. In our examination, we count it as mindfulness if we have established the heedful mind from the beginning when handling some business, and we count it as unmindfulness if we have lost the heedful mind. This examination is repeated continuously until we have made it our habit to mobilize the heedful mind in all things.

The next stage involves examining whether the results of our actions have turned out well or badly. If, as described above, heedfulness has become our standard in nearly all things as we look for presence or absence with the heedful mind, then the next stage is to examine how good or poor the results of those things are. In other words, we count it as mindfulness if the results of our dealings are good, and unmindfulness if they turn out poorly. In the process, we increase the chances of producing good results as we handle our affairs.

As we establish our ability with this mindfulness practice, the culmination of it is once again the realm of unmindfulness. It is only when we achieve this that we can truly rest easy.

Second, we apply ourselves to investigating and preparing in advance.

Unless we investigate and prepare in advance for all things, we will succumb to panic when we experience things, or we will miss the opportunities that present themselves. We will fail to distinguish wrong from right and act poorly, or we will choose that which our desires lead us to and bring disaster upon ourselves. In this way, we produce many side effects that lead us to failure in our endeavors.

For this reason, we should look closely at the things that will come in the future and take action to investigate them and prepare for them.

There is an old saying about this: We set the day's plan in the morning, we set the year's plan in the spring, and we set a lifetime's plan in our adolescence. The message in all of this is that we must predict the things that are to come and prepare for them. For the person who lacks this sense of preparation, no future is assured. He or she is forever unfortunate. Not only are such people unable to take a guiding role in development, they are also always simply trying to catch up with others. The odds are great that they will fail in all things.

They must practice in this way to instill the habit of preparing and make it a part of their character.

Third, we practice with the scriptures and laws.

The scriptures contain earnest loving-kindness, compassion, wisdom, and visions of the presiding buddhas. They do not compare to the writing that we ordinary humans have produced with our minds of discriminating consciousness. All laws also contain within them norms for community living. For us to try to live in ignorance of them is neither wisdom nor an effective means of living in this world.

No matter how good something may be, we do not experience its grace if we do not understand and put that thing to use. The scriptures are a jewel beyond price, incomparable to any of the jewels that fill the world systems of the trichiliocosm. All laws are norms that stand before us alongside the scriptures, seeking to prevent disaster and open the gateway of blessings to us. How auspicious it is, and what a blessing, when we study and practice them from up close, making and using them as our own!

We must spend much time with the scriptures and the laws, for the ultimate stage that we reach will be one in which all the myriad of phenomena of the universe and the empty dharma realm are used as true scriptures.

Fourth, we investigate cases for questioning.

In the scriptures, cases for questioning are described as the keys to awakening. Whatever those who feel no need for awakening may do, someone who intends to achieve awakening needs to regard cases for questioning as essential and carry them with him or her always.

In truth, our awareness of issues is greater the higher our order among animals, and the higher our spiritual capacity. In our lives, we are never content with reality; we are constantly envisioning new dimensions. And so we seek to find the nature of the issue that confronts us, and we anguish over how to solve it. This is what is meant by a case for questioning. It may be questioning related to human affairs, or it may be questioning about universal principles. The deeper we sink into our case for questioning, the greater the awakening is when it comes.

There is another saying: "After agonizing comes inspiration." In our lives, we may often have the experience of agonizing night and day over what to do about something, only to suddenly find a decisive solution. "Aha! That's it," we say. It is an example of the inspiration and wisdom that we gain after agonizing over a case for questioning.

Thus, cases for questioning are the ground from which wisdom is born, and the key to awakening. Sometimes, people will confess to me that "the case for questioning isn't taking hold." They are admitting this to me simply because they think of the case for questioning as something vague, or they lack the sense of enterprise. If we view each thought with reason, then everything—be it human affairs, universal principles, the things that we see and hear—is absolutely material for questioning. In the scriptures, and in the objects that surround us, we find an abundance of material to question.

In Buddhism, the 1,200 koans were presented as *hwadus* for questioning. Yet even these are of no use to one who does not try. We must accept these cases for questioning as material for practice, considering them and investigating them.

Fifth, we cultivate ourselves by reciting the Buddha's name and performing seated meditation in the morning and evening.

Reciting the Buddha's name and performing seated meditation are specialized methods of practice for removing distracting thoughts and nurturing the one mind. They are also indirect methods of practice for removing the wrong and nurturing the right.

Explanations about reciting the Buddha's name and seated meditation are already provided in the *Principal Book*, and commentaries have been published on them. Here, I will just elaborate on reciting the Buddha's name, performing seated meditation, and other special subjects for nurturing the power of concentration.

When a person spends time concentrating on something, thoughts about other things and idle thoughts have nowhere to enter. The question of how much power we have to concentrate, however, is a matter of skill. This skill differs from one circumstance to another. In general, we can speak of one form of concentration through the influence of external conditions, and another that is formed through our own subjective effort. The first type of concentration comes about naturally from external demands or stimuli as we are faced with something of interest or a crisis. This enables us to develop or to resolve our problems, manifesting its effects in the course of action we take and the problem with which we are faced. This effect, however, is only observed in the scope of those real-world demands.

The other form of concentration is achieved through subjective efforts, and specifically through reciting the Buddha's name and performing seated meditation. The recitation or meditation itself does not have the attraction or power to guide us into strong concentration. Rather, we ourselves are driving our concentration, pushing it toward the target of the recitation or meditation. This is how we nurture our fundamental power of concentration. The concentration that we gain from this manifests its effects as we apply it to each situation in which it is needed. This concentration is the mother of all success, and so we must nurture it by reciting the Buddha's name and performing seated meditation in our daily life.

Sixth, we examine our daily routine to observe all the items we need to develop and those we need to forsake.

In our lives as human beings, there are certain things that we must do and others that we must not do. We also speak of "recommendations" and "prohibitions." They exist both in religious terms and in ethical ones. They are present in social norms and in our practice. They are there in life and there in the process of proceeding toward some goal.

In all of these cases, the things that we must do represent the "right," and the things that we must not do represent the "wrong." It is only when we put both into practice that we achieve development and produce grace. Only by carrying out the things that must be done do we produce development and grace. Conversely, it is only when we refrain completely from the things that we must not do that we can prevent harm and produce development and grace.

Yet we cannot carry on this practice unless these things become habit and part of our character. If we have practiced once, we must not relax and think that we are finished, having done that. We must examine and examine more so that it becomes completely a matter of habit, and we must commit ourselves sincerely and tenaciously until it becomes part of our character.

What we must not do is practice once and believe that we are done, or become impatient and anguish when our practice does not happen right away.

Let us examine this in the form of a diagram:

Main Principles of Zen

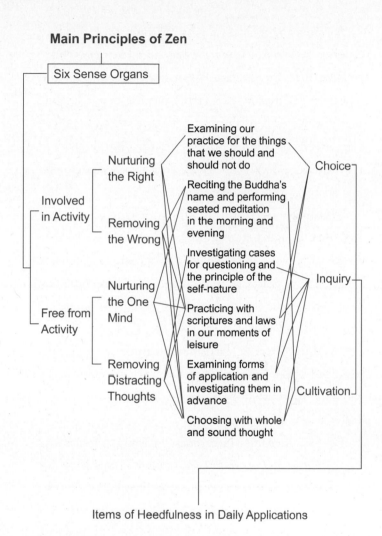

Six Sense Organs

Involved in Activity

Free from Activity

Nurturing the Right

Removing the Wrong

Nurturing the One Mind

Removing Distracting Thoughts

Examining our practice for the things that we should and should not do

Reciting the Buddha's name and performing seated meditation in the morning and evening

Investigating cases for questioning and the principle of the self-nature

Practicing with scriptures and laws in our moments of leisure

Examining forms of application and investigating them in advance

Choosing with whole and sound thought

Choice

Inquiry

Cultivation

Items of Heedfulness in Daily Applications

Disciplining is a matter of pursuing the effects of repeated action. This is why we use the term "discipline" to describe our practice; we are attempting to gain awesome abilities by repeatedly putting our discipline into practice. It is by no means a matter that is resolved through one or two instances of practice. We simply need the attitude of deeply instilling a determination to *do, do, and do again until it happens by itself.*

The only way to do this is by reviewing whether we practiced or not before going to sleep every night. In the process, we urge ourselves to continue further with what we have practiced, and to exert ourselves with great determination on what we have not practiced, showing a newfound commitment to it.

If we approach it with the commitment doing one hundred times what others have done once, and a thousand times what others have done ten times, then it will open up for us without fail.

The Six Items of Heedfulness in Daily Applications are a process that we must pass through in our daily life, whatever our practice may be. The dharma of practice in *Won*-Buddhism presents watertight measures for this by giving us the diary dharmas (fixed-term and daily) for examining our practice of this.

The proper sequence for someone who seeks to

practice the dharma of Timeless Zen by removing distracting thoughts and nurturing the one mind, and by removing the wrong and nurturing the right, is to begin straight away with practicing the Six Items of Heedfulness in Daily Applications. This is a practice that will guarantee results.

CHAPTER FIVE

THE DHARMA OF TIMELESS ZEN AND THE ITEMS OF HEEDFULNESS REGARDING TEMPLE VISITS

The skilled practitioner of the dharma of Timeless Zen is the one who lives his or her life relying on the temple for things related to faith and dharma. The temple is like a faucet, supplying the wisdom and the great loving-kindness and compassion of the buddhas and bodhisattvas. Faith and dharma are the pathways by which this wisdom, this great loving-kindness and compassion of the buddhas and bodhisattvas, is supplied to us like water from a faucet. Without them, we may experience the tathāgata's wisdom, loving-kindness, and compassion indirectly, but we will never have a direct supply—not because they are not supplied, but because we block the supply ourselves.

There is a proverb that says, "We die when our pulse fails." The practitioner who is cut off from the pulse of faith and the pulse of dharma will see the life force in his or her practice die off as well. This then becomes a limitation.

This is why we are told, "When we awaken yet have no faith, the only things that grow are distorted views."

But we often see cases where the practitioner becomes arrogant, believing that his or her practice is complete after a small bit of realization or understanding, and teachers and the spirit of faith alike fall away as the practitioner imagines himself or herself as a "lone general." Having achieved awakening does not mean that we have also become balanced or right in commanding our true nature. In these cases, we have created and succumbed to our own limitations in our practice. How can we ever attain the realm of practicing hand in hand with the buddhas and bodhisattvas, or of sharing in half the dharma seat?

When we visit the temple, when we search for teachers and colleagues in the dharma, we must engage in questions and answers, using our experiences as material. We must obtain appraisals for what we have sensed, and we must ask about our doubts and gain the awakening of understanding. We must also take part in fixed-term training and perform specialized practice as we attend regular and other dharma meetings, and we must commit ourselves sincerely to actually using what we have gained from our practice.

There is a trap to which the practitioner is susceptible after a long period of visiting temples, and that is the idea that he or she has already heard everything there is to hear. When caught by this mistaken notion, we constantly think that everything is the same old thing—that we know it all. We grow bored, and we feel that we have heard it all, heard it over and over again until we finally become annoyed with it, and our desire to attend more dharma meetings slowly diminishes.

At this point, we drift farther and farther away from the dharma without realizing it, and we are drawn into the midst of worldly concerns. Once there, it is not easy for us to find our way back. This is evidence that we have entered the path of regression.

If we think of our attendance of regular dharma meetings, however half-hearted, as simply a part of daily life, and if we make the effort to gain something from them, however small, then it is certain that we *will* gain something.

One passage from a dharma instruction is enough for us to change the course of our life. Simply from seeing the Dharmakaya Buddha and meeting colleagues, we gain a deepening of our buddha affinity. How could we ever complain that we are gaining nothing from dharma meetings?

Practitioner of Timeless Zen will only gain great help in their practice of Timeless Zen when they regard attending dharma meetings as an ironclad rule in their temple visits, when they deeply instill the Six Items of Heedfulness in their Temple Visits, and when these items are present in their practice.

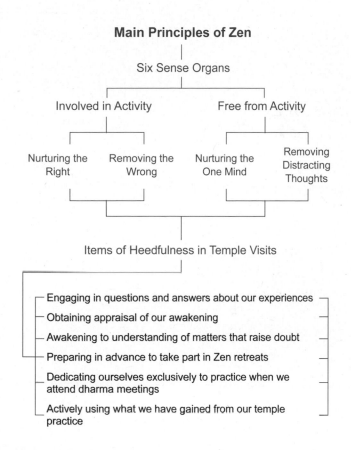

Main Principles of Zen

Six Sense Organs

Involved in Activity — Free from Activity

Nurturing the Right — Removing the Wrong — Nurturing the One Mind — Removing Distracting Thoughts

Items of Heedfulness in Temple Visits

- Engaging in questions and answers about our experiences
- Obtaining appraisal of our awakening
- Awakening to understanding of matters that raise doubt
- Preparing in advance to take part in Zen retreats
- Dedicating ourselves exclusively to practice when we attend dharma meetings
- Actively using what we have gained from our temple practice

CHAPTER SIX

THE DHARMA OF TIMELESS ZEN
AND THE QUICKEST EXPEDIENT
TO ATTAINING THE THREE
GREAT POWERS IN BOTH ACTION
AND REST

P art Two of the "Practice" chapter in the *Scripture of the Founding Master* is a dharma instruction on the quickest expedient to attaining the three great powers in both action and rest. "In both action and rest" means that the instruction applies equally when we are involved in activity and when we are free from activity, while "the quickest expedient to attaining the three great powers" refers to none other than the dharma of Timeless Zen. Given that this dharma instruction was given to us directly by the Founding Master, it cannot be omitted from any commentary on the dharma of Timeless Zen.

The Founding Master presents us with two paths for each form of the Threefold Study in both action and rest. All of them are also ways of generating the result of removing distracting thoughts and nurturing the one mind, and of removing the wrong and nurturing the right. Because it ties in with this context, I present the following diagram. It specifies the quickest expedient and should therefore serve as a major reference for the practitioner.

Main Principles of Zen

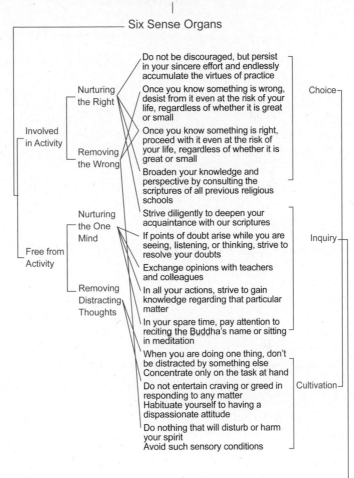

Six Sense Organs

Involved in Activity

Nurturing the Right

Removing the Wrong

- Do not be discouraged, but persist in your sincere effort and endlessly accumulate the virtues of practice
- Once you know something is wrong, desist from it even at the risk of your life, regardless of whether it is great or small
- Once you know something is right, proceed with it even at the risk of your life, regardless of whether it is great or small
- Broaden your knowledge and perspective by consulting the scriptures of all previous religious schools

Choice

Free from Activity

Nurturing the One Mind

Removing Distracting Thoughts

- Strive diligently to deepen your acquaintance with our scriptures
- If points of doubt arise while you are seeing, listening, or thinking, strive to resolve your doubts
- Exchange opinions with teachers and colleagues
- In all your actions, strive to gain knowledge regarding that particular matter
- In your spare time, pay attention to reciting the Buddha's name or sitting in meditation

Inquiry

- When you are doing one thing, don't be distracted by something else Concentrate only on the task at hand
- Do not entertain craving or greed in responding to any matter Habituate yourself to having a dispassionate attitude
- Do nothing that will disturb or harm your spirit Avoid such sensory conditions

Cultivation

The quickest expedient to attain the three great powers in both action and rest

CHAPTER SEVEN

THE DHARMA OF TIMELESS ZEN AND INTERNAL AND EXTERNAL PURITY AND QUIESCENCE

P art Nine in the "Practice" chapter of the *Scripture of the Founding Master* shares the practice dharma of internal and external purity and quiescence. This refers to our having achieved purity and quiescence both internally and externally, with an inner and outer correspondence of purity and quiescence achieved through being pure inwardly, and purity and quiescence achieved through being unmoving outwardly.

We are only truly healthy in our bodies when we are healthy both inside and out. Very often, we may be the healthy on the outside, but acquire external diseases when inner diseases arise, or we may healthy on the inside, but have an external ailment that arises and spreads within. In Chinese medicine, they speak of "assorted diseases from internal injuries" and "miscellaneous diseases from external sensations." The same is true for diseases of our mind.

Sometimes, shocks from outside ourselves enter within to rattle our purity and quiescence. At other times, it is internal turbulence that reaches and shakes our external purity and quiescence. Strictly speaking, then, "inner" and "outer" are not separate. We therefore require discipline both in internal and external purity and quiescence.

This purity and quiescence is the thing that we practitioners greatly thirst for. For it is through purity and quiescence that we can produce wisdom, produce grace, and gain the powers of liberation and self-control.

We should therefore look more closely at what is meant by purity and quiescence.

In the *Great Learning*, we find a passage that reads, The point where to rest being known, the object of pursuit is then determined; that having been determined, a calm unperturbedness may be attained. That calmness will followed by a tranquil repose. In that repose there may be careful deliberation, and that deliberation will be followed by the attainment of the desired goal.

This teaching is a dharma instruction that effectively shows the unfolding process from the beginning of purity and quiescence to its result. Because the conclusion of purity and quiescence is the attainment of awareness or of the desired end, failures in our purity or quiescence will make it impossible to guarantee the outcome of attaining awareness or our desired goal.

By way of explanation, the message is that we must find and understand where to stop and abide if we are to achieve stability and settle down; it is only when we have properly settled then that the wandering and unstable mind will rest and achieve tranquility; it is only when the spirit is tranquil that we achieve ultimate comfort; it is only when we have comfort of the spirit that we can think with one mind; and the attainment of awakening or the desired goal comes from thought that is of the one mind. Purity and quiescence are thus the foundation of achieving the fruits of practice.

The practitioner is therefore obliged to pass through the gateway of purity and quiescence.

To achieve this, it is essential to discipline ourselves with internal and external purity and quiescence in both action and rest in accordance with the following diagram.

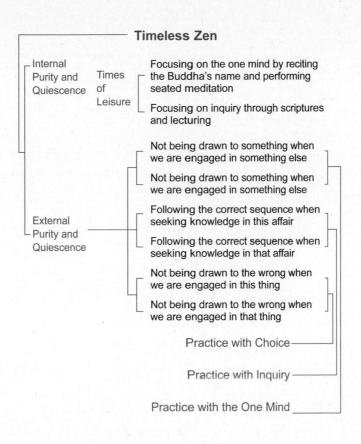

Timeless Zen

Internal Purity and Quiescence — Times of Leisure
- Focusing on the one mind by reciting the Buddha's name and performing seated meditation
- Focusing on inquiry through scriptures and lecturing

External Purity and Quiescence
- Not being drawn to something when we are engaged in something else
- Not being drawn to something when we are engaged in something else
- Following the correct sequence when seeking knowledge in this affair
- Following the correct sequence when seeking knowledge in that affair
- Not being drawn to the wrong when we are engaged in this thing
- Not being drawn to the wrong when we are engaged in that thing

Practice with Choice

Practice with Inquiry

Practice with the One Mind

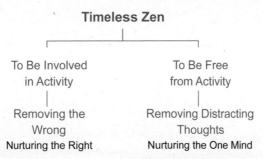

Timeless Zen

To Be Involved in Activity

Removing the Wrong
Nurturing the Right

To Be Free from Activity

Removing Distracting Thoughts
Nurturing the One Mind

CHAPTER EIGHT

TIMELESS ZEN AND THE TRANSMISSION VERSES ON CULTIVATING THE MIND

The Transmission Verses on Cultivating the Mind are a good depiction of the process of Timeless Zen practice. By listing them here, I hope to provide a reference for the practitioner.

1. Before Taming

This is the completely unpolished state. There are no constraints of self-rule or rule by others. It is the stage of the free-wheeling life, of romping this way and that, of striking against this thing and the other, or causing only harm and injury to ourselves and others according to our thoughts, according to our moods, according to our greed, hatred, and delusion.

2. At the Beginning of Taming

This is the time when the constraints of self-rule and rule by others have begun. We have begun our polishing by applying controls through rightful laws, rules, and principles, but the wild, solidified habits of the past continue to rage, causing strain and anguish to ourselves and others.

3. In the Process of Taming

This is the time when we have started experiencing the controls of self-rule and rule by others. We have just entered the state of accepting control from ourselves and others, so we follow as we are led. But because of the habits and karmic power underlying our mind, it is a stage for receiving stronger controls and pulling the reins tighter.

4. Turning the Head

This is the stage where we have returned to the right path through the controls of ourselves and others and the virtues of exertion and accumulating merits, but we still cannot release the mind. We must be all the more wary, making sure to hold the reins of the mind and not let go.

5. Becoming Tamed

This is the stage where we have submitted completely to the guidance of our taming. The power of autonomy, of doing as we understand, has established itself in us, and we have become yielding to the controls of self-rule and rule by others, so that we are almost never bothered by them.

6. Freedom from Obstructions

This is the stage where we experience neither enticements nor obstructions in acting in accordance with the dharma. We merely proceed with a foundation in the dharma, so that everything obstructing disappears, the strain of self-rule and rule by others comes to an end, and our subjectivity and objectivity are tranquil and we enjoy comfortable bliss in the Way.

7. Leisure

This is the stage of releasing the mind to nature. We are giving the mind over to wherever it will flow. When we are hungry, we eat; when we are thirsty, we drink; when we are tired, we rest. We have entrusted all things, yet the danger of defying regulations has vanished, so that the subject who is observing has no work to do.

8. Forgetting Each Other

This is the stage where both ability (subjectivity) and objects (objectivity) have come to rest. Both the object that is being tamed and the subject who does the taming have finished their business and merely enjoy the origin of tranquility with thought, will, or purpose. All intervention has ceased.

9. Reflecting Alone

This is the stage where the object of taming disappears, leaving only the subject. It is the stage where the object that undergoes taming becomes one with the subject who tames, so that there is no separate object to tame. There is only the subject, who enjoys bliss of mind on its own and returns to the original home without action or traces.

10. Only the Il-Won-Sang Remains

In this realm, even the subject has disappeared, leaving only the true image that is perfectly round. All dharmas of effort vanish, and all this is revealed is the original true image that transcends subjectivity and objectivity, the ability to transform or to be transformed. It is a stage of replete wisdom, the stage of having ascended to the unequaled realm.

CHAPTER NINE

TIMELESS ZEN AND RESTING IN THE ELIXIR FIELD

When we are involved in activity, the reality of removing the wrong and nurturing the right must be present. When we are free from activity, the reality of removing distracting thoughts and nurturing the one mind must be present. The commentary thus far is an explanation of how to achieve this.

Because there is already an existing *Commentary on the Methods of Seated Meditation*, I have omitted a specific explanation of the specialized practice for nurturing the one mind when we are free from activity. We must also be ever calm in alertness and ever alert in calmness but also ever exact in persistence and ever persistent in exactitude.

By way of explanation, this means that our spirit as we practice meditation should be calm in the midst of its alertness and alert in the midst of its calmness. We must also be exact as we persist and persist, and persist and persist while remaining exact.

The alert spirit is that which does not succumb to the demon of drowsiness, while the calm spirit is that which is not swayed by idle thoughts. The persisting and persisting mind is the mind without interruptions, and the exact mind is the state of mind that is replete with the one mind.

These two things are things that we must cling to and wrestle with to the last in our practice of meditation. The practitioner must take them deeply to heart and strive with them to the end.

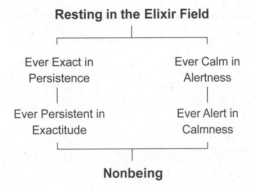

CONCLUSION

This concludes my commentary on the dharma of Timeless Zen. I have kept it short to minimize the burden on the reader, but I also feel many regrets about not providing a more detailed guide.

Because the dharma of Timeless Zen is not theory, however, and because personal practice is so important, I believe that even what I have shared thus far will serve as a guide for practicing Timeless Zen.

Yet despite the fact that the practice of the dharma of Timeless Zen is something that the whole world needs, there are still very few who seek to practice it, and there are many who do it as an adjunct, so that they roam about without finding the right way. How unfortunate this is!

Last year, I traveled around Sydney, Australia, and Auckland, New Zealand. Nowhere I went did I see any garbage; no homes were surrounded by large fences or barred by gates. The way that they lived was the very picture of peacefulness.

If merely achieving that level of national consciousness

were enough to create something like paradise, imagine how great each country and society would be if all people practice to remove the wrong and nurture the right, and to remove distracting thoughts and nurture the one mind!

This dharma of Timeless Zen is not a practice that only special people can perform. Anyone can do it—all you have to be is a human being. It is something that we should deeply consider, not only in terms of managing our character as individuals but also from the standpoints of the humanities, of the social sciences, of national policy.

If every member of society were to start practicing this way in earnest, it would be a great cause for celebration in the future of each individual and in the future of the home, society, the nation, and the world. A world would come into being where no prisons were needed; this world would be a world of buddhas and bodhisattvas.

Moreover, this dharma of Timeless Zen is not a practice that takes us away from our work and duties. It is a practice for when we are in the midst of any part of our daily life, and so it is a practice that can be recommended to everyone and that everyone should be encouraged to do. At the same time, its effects are manifested right away in our affairs and in our practice. We truly have no reason to hesitate or delay.

The whole world should engage in the practice of

Timeless Zen. We should start at this very moment. If we do so, good fortune awaits us. A paradise-like world will greet us.

At the same time, the dharma of Timeless Zen is also a practical matter, and it should be approached realistically. It is not at all some empty play of concepts. If we describe our actions as "practicing Timeless Zen" but do not remove distracting thoughts and wrong from our practice or nurture the one mind and the right, then the skills that we gain from that practice will be lacking. The dharma of Timeless Zen is a practical issue, and we must perform it practically time after time. If we do that, then we will experience for ourselves the most astonishing effects from the moment that we begin.

Credits

Author	Prime Dharma Master Emeritus Chwasan
Translator	Colin Mouat
Publisher	Kim Hyung-geun
Editor	Lee Jin-hyuk
Copy Editor	Gary Rector
Proofreader	Jaime Stief
Designer	Jung Hyun-young